THE
KINGDOM
FOR THE
KINGLESS

Craig A. Smith

THE
KINGDOM
FOR THE
KINGLESS

Learning to live as
ambassadors of the
now-and-coming King

Shepherd Project Press

Shepherd Project Press
91 South Carlton Street
Castle Rock, CO 80104
Email: spp@shepherdproject.com

Shepherd Project Press is the publishing division of Shepherd Project Ministries, a Christian para-church organization dedicated to training and equipping the followers of Jesus for radical Kingdom living.

All Scripture quotations, unless otherwise indicated, are taken from the NEW AMERICAN STANDARD BIBLE®,Copyright © 1960,1962,1963,1968,1971,1972,1973,1975,1977,1995 by The Lockman Foundation. Used by permission.

ISBN 0-9755135-0-8

Printed in the United States of America

ACKNOWLEDGEMENTS

I am deeply indebted to many individuals for their assistance on this project: to the faculty and staff of Denver Seminary who first forced me to wrestle with the then-ridiculous notion of the now-and-coming; to my many listeners over the years who have heard these developing ideas in their least polished forms; to my dear friends and editors, Dr. Brent Kinman, Elizabeth Roth, Karen Tate, and Ramon Padilla; to my family for all their encouragement and support over the years. Most of all, to my bride, Coletta, whose contributions could never be captured in these few words but without whose support none of this would have been possible.

CONTENTS

A Note To The Reader

Much like the Kingdom of God itself, this book has invaded my life in unexpected and wonderful ways. If they are also, at times, disconcerting, that is simply the rose's thorn.

I did not really intend to write a book on this subject, but as is so often the case, my intentions proved shockingly irrelevant.

It has hardly been convenient. As I write these words, I have an unfinished doctoral dissertation weighing heavily on my mind. I have lectures to prepare, sermons to think about, seminars to schedule and a host of other obligations pressing around, demanding my attention. And they should have it…after all, they were all on the schedule.

This book, on the other hand, was very much an unscheduled appointment. I have agreed to it only reluctantly and in stages. Several years ago, the subject began to jump out at me from just about every page in Scripture. Over time, I became convinced that needed to be addressed. My schedule wasn't clear enough to address it then, I pleaded, but I would get around to it as soon as possible.

Incessant knocking finally persuaded me to open the door a bit and I agreed to make time for a short visit, perhaps to be expanded upon at a more convenient time. I had been following the remarkable popularity of Bruce Wilkinson's book, *The*

Prayer of Jabez, somewhat surprised that such a small work could find such a large audience. From the perspective of length, *The Prayer of Jabez* isn't really a book so *much as it is a long essay. Perhaps Wilkinson is on to something,* I thought. *Perhaps the essay, long out of style, is making a comeback.*

An extended essay, I decided, was something I could handle. Something on the order of 80 or 90 pages of reasonably large text with generous line-spacing would be about right. Just enough to raise awareness about a critically important issue without getting too bogged down in theological details.

You will notice, of course, that what you now hold in your hands does not precisely fit that description. The font is somewhat smaller than I anticipated and the line spacing not nearly so generous as I originally envisioned. In spite of this, the anticipated eighty or ninety-page benchmark was transgressed some time ago and is quickly receding into the distance.

Still, I have tried hard to make this book two things: short and accessible. Those readers already familiar with some of the theological intricacies related to the Kingdom of God may find this work lacking in detail. I am well aware that, in places, the book skims quickly over very deep waters. For example, while we will touch briefly on the relationship between the Christian Church and the nation of Israel, we will not spend much time on this complex subject.

This is an intentional decision. *The Kingdom For The Kingless* is supposed to be a sort of primer, an introduction to a theme that is absolutely central to the Bible but about which many Christians today are unfortunately naïve: the Kingdom of God. We use the term on occasion, but it appears that we do not really know what it is. This is tragic, for apart from an adequate understanding of the Kingdom, we can never fully understand what it means to be made in the Image of God, what victory the gospel truly proclaims, or what hope heaven really holds.

Other readers, perhaps those less familiar with some of the debates and discussions that often occupy Christian scholars, may find the waters here quite deep enough, thank you very much. And that is as it should be. We may *skim*, but I hope no one finds us *glossing*. Many a casual reader will, no doubt, find that this book deals with subjects they have scarcely heard about, let alone contemplated. For such readers, I have tried to "keep it casual," as they say. In the deeper waters I will ask everyone to dip their toes at least, but I do not intend to dunk them unexpectedly. The language is light, the analogies and illustrations plentiful, and some of the fiercer and more complicated debates are set on the back burner for now. I have kept the footnotes to a minimum, primarily using them to touch briefly on the unavoidable questions that more technical readers will simply not allow me to bypass entirely. This is not an academic theology book, but it is, after all, about deep matters.

Part of the length of this book is due to my decision to include in the text many of the Scripture passages being cited. Since this book quotes extensively from the Bible, I could have shortened it somewhat by simply citing the relevant passages. However, if you are anything at all like me, this probably wouldn't happen. Since it is so critical that my readers see that what I am saying here is not a clever interpretation of Scripture, but rather its clear teaching, I thought it best to include the actual text of the Bible in many places. I trust you will find this a help and not a hindrance.

I can envision no greater satisfaction than if, when you have finished this book, you lay it aside and think to yourself, "Of course. How obvious." I imagine that few of my readers will have ever conceived of the Christian life in precisely these terms, but I hope that when they are done, they will be genuinely surprised that they have not already have seen what was really so obvious. But this is often the case, as has been so frequently demonstrated in my own life.

As Edward R. Murrow once said: "The obscure we see eventually. The completely obvious, it seems, takes longer."

Right Thinking Precedes Right Living

In one sense, this is not a *practical* book. In another sense, though, it is the most practical sort of book you are ever likely to read.

This is not a "self-help" book or a guided tour to personal improvement. There are no "seven steps to a better marriage" or "five characteristics of a godly dad" in here. If that is what is meant by a book being "practical," then this is not a practical book.

However, I have long been convinced of something that often gets ignored in our day and age: *right thinking precedes right living.* What I mean is that truly significant change in our lives always flows out of changes in the way we think about who we are and what we are supposed to be doing.   Mere cognitive recognition is not, of course, all that is required for significant growth, but it is an indispensable *starting point.* Changes in behavior without an accompanying change in our underlying thinking are always short-lived.

Such changes are like trying to shim up the Tower of Pisa. You remember the Tower of Pisa, right? Begun in 1173, the Tower was supposed to be a grand structure that inspired awe in everyone who saw it. Unfortunately, they built it on mushy ground. Because it sits on inadequate foundations, the Tower has begun to lean dangerously and will eventually fall.

Imagine, however, that some enterprising engineer comes up with a system of wires that are attached to the Tower of Pisa. Each wire is then run through pullies anchored to another building or to a great spike in the ground several hundred yards away. With a great deal of fanfare and a lot of horsepower, the wires snap taut and the tower begins to groan...and then, behold! The leaning Tower of Pisa leans no more! It stands perfectly straight. This would be an impressive display of engineering skill, no doubt, but let me ask you this: who would move their business offices into the tower? No one, of course, because the moment the tension is released on all those cables and pullies, the tower will start leaning again...probably more so than before. Without a radical repair to the foundation, the slow fall will resume.

Anyone who has ever tried to break a bad habit, without really being convinced in their hearts that the habit needed to be broken, knows exactly what I'm talking about here. Like the Tower of Pisa, true change in our lives can only proceed from alterations to the foundations. And, in this case of this book, the foundations relate to right thinking about the Kingdom of God.

I suppose that a book on the Kingdom of God could be built around "Five Characteristics of a Kingdom Builder" or "Eight Habits of Kingdom-Minded People" or something similar, but that is really not what this book is about. This book deals with issues and ideas that ultimately form the very foundation of what it means to be human. Everything that we do rests upon, and flows from, this foundation. Sometimes we are conscious of the ways in which our foundational beliefs affect what we do and sometimes we are not. Whether we are conscious or unconscious of them, however, such effects are irresistible.

The Kingdom And The Image of God

In the first chapter of Genesis, a provocative statement is made. It is a statement which has the potential to utterly change the way our understanding of who we are and why we exist. It is a statement with which you are probably familiar:

> Then God said, "Let Us make man in Our image, according to Our likeness..."
>
> (Genesis 1:26-27)

Most Christians are well-acquainted with this verse. This notion of being made in the "image of God" is something that most of us have encountered on many occasions. Unfortunately, most of us have no real idea what we're talking about when we use the phrase. And the reason that we don't really know what it means to be made in the *Image* of God, is that we don't know what the *Kingdom* of God is[1]. As we will soon see, the doctrine of human beings as made in God's Image is intricately connected to the Kingdom of God theme that runs from Genesis to Revelation.

It is significant that the above-quoted passage occurs at the very beginning of the Bible. It stands to reason that if we fail to get this fact straight right from the start, then much of what follows will be incomprehensible.

There are actually two major theological assertions to be found in the first chapter of Genesis. The first is that God is the sovereign Creator of all that exists. The second is that human beings are made in His Image. If we misunderstand either of

---

[1] A friend of mine pointed out that this statement could be taken to mean that Old Testament prophets, such as Moses, whose understanding of the Kingdom was necessarily incomplete, could not have understood what it meant to be made in the Image of God. I do not believe that to be the case. While Moses' understanding of the Kingdom of God was certainly incomplete, since much of its nature was yet to be revealed, I think he knew quite well what kingdoms in general were and what it meant to call God King. Consequently, I believe he understood precisely what it meant to say that humans had been made in the Image of God.

these truths, we will never be able to understand the rest of the Bible's message. These truths are foundational to our ability to encounter God's Word as it is meant to be encountered.

If our understanding of what it means to be human, made in the Image of God, is *correct*, then our lives will reflect the firmness of our foundation. If, on the other hand, our foundations are flawed, everything we build on top of them will teeter and totter and come crashing down around us at the worst possible times.

Unfortunately, my experience has been that most Christians have an inadequate, if not fundamentally flawed, understanding of what it means to be made in the Image of God. Misunderstandings abound. On the one hand, some have an overly-inflated view of themselves, misunderstanding the *Imago Dei*[2] to mean that they are presently, or at least *potentially*, equals with God. This particular misunderstanding goes all the way back to the Garden, where Satan first suggested it to Adam and Eve.

On the other hand, many, if not most, people have a radically under-inflated view of what the *Imago Dei* means. They have reduced it to mean nothing more than the possession of a dry list of abilities and attributes such as the capacity for moral reflection and rational thought.

Both of these errors provide inadequate foundations for living the lives for which we were made. However, when we properly understand the "big picture" of biblical teaching on what it means to be human – that is, when our understanding of the *Imago Dei* is firmly and rightly established – how we live our lives will be fundamentally transformed in ways that lists of "five characteristics" and "seven steps" can never accomplish.

---

[2] The term used in theological discussions about being made in the Image of God.

Putting It Into Practice

In that sense, returning now to the original point I wanted to make, this book is *imminently* practical because we cannot begin to understand the Kingdom of God without finding new light shed on other critical doctrines that will radically impact the way we live our lives.

As I have already said, this book does not contain a great deal of "do this" and "do that" sort of advice. In part, this is because I think it far more effective to get at the foundations than to concentrate on the manifestations.

There is another reason, however, and it is this: you don't need them. Let me explain: As a human being made in God's Image, you possess the dignity and capacity necessary to see the implications of the ideas in this book. If you will read carefully and be sensitive to the leading of the Holy Spirit, you will see the practical applications which specifically relate to you.

If are lives are like houses, let me warn you: I'm not an interior designer and this book is not about interior decoration. You have to make the house your own and I would not presume to tell you what shades you should paint it or how you should arrange your furniture. This book deals with architectural and structural integrity. My job is to help you make sure your house is built well on firm foundations. My task is to challenge some of your underlying thinking and help you to see where some changes may need to be made.

Shall we begin the renovations?

ONE

The Forgotten Kingdom

Even the most familiar thing, left alone long enough, become novel again.

Take a deep breath and hold it. Hold it until it becomes uncomfortable. Hold it until your lungs are crying out. Then, when you can't wait any longer, exhale slowly. Now, very deliberately, draw in a lung-full of fresh air.

You may notice things about that first delicious breath that you've long forgotten: how sweet it is, how invigorating. You may notice its flavor, its texture, and its nuances in ways that you've never before been aware of.

This is what I mean when I say that familiar things can become novel again, if left alone for long enough.

Virginia Wolf once wrote: *"You can't go home again."* She's right; not because home is no longer there, but because the single-most important characteristic of home is familiarity. What makes home *home* is the fact that it is familiar in deep and abiding ways. It is precisely those moments in our childhood when change or unfamiliarity enter our lives that we feel most threatened, because our sense of *familiarity* is undermined and, with it, our sense of *home.*

But go away for a while…say to college or to start a career, and you can never quite recapture that all-important sense of familiarity again. It may be the same house and the same objects and the same people who fill it, but it will be profoundly different because your perception of it has changed. It is no longer familiar in the same way and so it is no longer *home* in the sense that it once was.

Of course, this is not necessarily a bad thing. With the loss of familiarity we may begin to see things in new ways and to savor them with a new appreciation. Familiarity, while comforting, can also have an anesthetic effect on us. Its loss may therefore allow us new feelings and understandings of the once-familiar object. A pleasant holiday meal spent with our parents in our childhood home is often far sweeter than any of the countless repasts of our youth.

Novel Or New?

What I want to say in this book may appear novel to some readers for precisely the same reason. In certain Christian circles, this topic has been neglected in recent years. Indeed, for some of you it will not only appear to be novel, it will actually be *new*. You may never have heard the Christian life and faith described in quite this light. Let me assure you that what I will say here is not new in any significant way, but is only a once-familiar teaching which has grown novel again through inattention.

This book is about the Kingdom of God. The Kingdom of God is often misunderstood today, because it is not one of the central themes emphasized by contemporary Christian teaching. This is profoundly ironic given the fact that, as we shall soon see, it is one of the most dominant motifs, not only of the Gospels and the New Testament, but of the entire Bible. The theme of the Kingdom of God extends from the first chapter of Genesis to the last words of John's Revelation. The Kingdom is the absolute cornerstone of Jesus' teaching. Apart from an adequate understanding of the Kingdom, we can never fully understand what it means to be made as the Image of God, what the gospel proclaims or what heaven holds.

The Kingdom As An Integrating Motif

Let me be pointed: I am suggesting that the Kingdom of God is what biblical scholars sometimes call an "integrating motif," a theme around which the larger witness of Scripture organizes itself. This theme provides a sort of interpretive key to understanding God's Word to us. An integrating motif is a big picture that provides a context for thinking about and relating the various different observations that emerge from a study of Scripture.

Over the years, many different integrating motifs have been suggested. Ultimately, the integrating motif that one focuses on defines the particular theological system that emerges from your study of Scripture. Some other integrating motifs which have formed the backbone of classic theological systems include: eras of God's interaction with humanity (Dispensationalism), God's absolute sovereignty (Calvinism or Reformed Theology) or divine sovereignty interacting with human freedom (Arminianism). Predictably, the emphasis on the Kingdom of God as an integrating motif in Scripture gives rise to a theological system known as Kingdom Theology.

I believe that Kingdom Theology is both the most comprehensive and consistent theological system that has ever been proposed. However, it has not enjoyed nearly the same popularity as some of the other systems. Almost everyone has heard of Calvinism, though they may not know what it really teaches. Dispensationalism has become so popular during the last hundred years or so that it is quite likely the dominant theological system in much of the United States. Even Arminianism has a great deal of "brand-name" recognition, though few people could tell you anything about the man for which it is named.

Kingdom Theology, on the other hand, has toiled along in relative obscurity for quite some time. Its biggest boost came through the work of George Eldon Ladd. Ladd is widely regarded as the founding father and leading proponent of Kingdom Theology. I believe, however, that he would have been quick to argue that he had not founded anything, but had merely called attention to an often misunderstood, but central, teaching of the Bible. Ladd had this to say about the Church's confusion:

> When we ask the Christian Church, "What is the Kingdom of God? When and how will it come?" we receive a bewildering diversity of explanations. There are few themes so prominent in the Bible which have received such radically divergent interpretations as that of the Kingdom of God.[3]

Ladd's work was, in many ways, a startling break from the dominant theological trends of his day. Unfortunately, some of Ladd's students have been accused of distorting their teacher's work and taking Kingdom Theology in an unhealthy direction[4]. In spite of this fact, Ladd's work constitutes an important contribution to evangelical theology and it is well worth reading. I was greatly influenced by Ladd's work, and this

---

[3] George Eldon Ladd. *The Gospel of the Kingdom.* (Grand Rapids: Eerdmans, 1959). 14.

[4] I am thinking here primarily of John Wimber, founder of the Vinyard movement which many evangelical leaders consider to have an unbiblical emphasis on signs and wonders. Wimber was a student of Ladd's at Fuller Seminary and seems to have been greatly influenced by his work on the Kingdom.

book will certainly show evidence of that influence. In spite of Ladd's influence, however, mention Kingdom Theology today and you are just as likely to get blank stares as anything else, because it remains a relatively obscure theological system, at least among the rank and file of Christians today. Within scholarly circles the system is much more widely known and often enjoys a great deal of respect, but much of the Christian world knows almost nothing about it.

Kingdom Theology And Eschatology

For some reason, when I do encounter people who have heard about Kingdom Theology, they often have a mistaken belief that it is connected to a particular eschatology (beliefs about the end times) called *postmillenialism*. Essentially, postmillenialism interprets Scripture to say that the Kingdom of God, as inaugurated by Jesus at his incarnation, crucifixion and resurrection, will continue to grow in influence throughout human history until it ushers in a metaphorical "reign" of Jesus. This will be a period in which the Church's influence in the world will produce an age of peace which will ultimately conclude with Jesus' physical return[5].

This view is something of a minority in Christian circles. By far the more common theological position throughout Church history has been *premillenialism*, which argues that the thousand year reign of peace *begins* with Jesus' return. In other words, while the Church continues to grow and influence

---

[5] By far the more common theological position throughout church history has been *premillenialism*, which argues that the thousand year reign of peace *begins* with Jesus' return. In other words, while the church continues to grow and influence the world, the general trend in world history is from bad to worse. This trend is only reversed with the Lord returns triumphantly.

the world, the general trend in history is from bad to worse. This trend is only reversed with the Lord returns triumphantly.

Now, this is not a book about eschatology, per-se, but I do not wish for any misguided associations to taint my reader's perception of its real subject. There is no particular reason to associate Kingdom Theology with postmillenialism. The relative obscurity of postmillenialism does not necessarily make it false, of course, but it means that postmillenialism is often viewed with great suspicion by much of the Christian Church. For this reason, when people associate Kingdom Theology with postmillenialism, they often tend to view Kingdom Theology with a great deal of skepticism.

So, let me lay my cards on the table: I do not hold to postmillenialism. I believe the Bible describes a personal, premillenial return of Jesus Christ to earth, at which point he will resurrect believers and usher in a literal thousand year reign of peace. This Millennium will then be followed by the resurrection of the unbelieving dead and the final judgment by God.

I make this overt statement of my end-times beliefs simply to avoid misunderstanding. Actually, there is no reason why Kingdom Theology need be associated with any particular eschatology at all. As a broad system of theology, it is not overly preoccupied with eschatology, or any other individual doctrine. Rather, Kingdom Theology seeks to draw some of the seemingly distinct sections of the Bible together around a central theme: the Kingdom of God. Of course, as such, Kingdom Theology will provide a sort of interpretive lens which will certainly affect the way we read certain texts and therefore, our understanding of particular doctrines which derive from those texts. Each theological system which is organized around an integrating motif naturally has certain doctrines that are of particular interest to it. Calvinism rather naturally focuses on the doctrines of providence (God's sovereignty) and soteriology (salvation). Dispensationalism spends a great deal of time on eschatology in particular. Kingdom Theology exerts its strongest influence on our formulation of the doctrines of Christian conduct, the nature and function of the Church and what it means to be made in the Image of God.

The Inclusiveness of Kingdom Theology

It is frequently assumed that any integrating motif in Scripture must be the *only* integrating motif, but I am not prepared to make such a blanket statement. Though they seek to be comprehensive systems, I believe that Dispensationalism, Calvinism, etc. are sometimes too narrow in their focus, so that they cannot adequately deal with elements of Scripture which do not quite fit inside their particular parameters. I do not wish to minimize the important contributions of such systems, but I would like to suggest that none of these systems, taken individually, paint the whole picture.

Of course, the same may possibly be said of Kingdom Theology. There is more to the Bible and to God's unfolding plan in human history, than can be described by any one system. However, having said that, I believe Kingdom Theology does offer a more comprehensive and biblical understanding of God's plan than any of the other systems. Moreover, I believe Kingdom Theology may ultimately be broad enough to include many of the theological contributions offered by the other major systems. There is no particular reason why you can't adhere to both Calvinism and Kingdom Theology or to some other combination. Kingdom Theology provides a context in which to understand the individual elements of God's unfolding plan of creation and redemption.

As I've said, Kingdom Theology is not widely known or taught today and this will make some of the ideas in this book sound new to many people. That perception could not be farther from the truth. In fact, the Kingdom of God was originally well-understood to be *the* central or integrating motif in Scripture. But, for various reasons, this focus on the Kingdom has been pushed aside.

In certain ways, Scripture's teaching on the Kingdom is like a favorite coat that has, for one reason or another, gone out of style. It has gradually found itself hidden away in the back of our closet, brought to light only in the occasional foray through our wardrobe as we come searching for something else.

The Kingdom of God has not been thrown out, only left alone. But because of this, I contend, Christians have often ventured into a cold world without the proper attire. It is time to bring it back out and to wrap ourselves anew in the warmth of its truth.

TWO

The Gospel Of The Kingdom

Ask the average American Christian what the gospel is and nine out of ten of them will get it wrong.

I have been in Christian ministry for a little over a decade now. I know that's not long. I know that I am only beginning to walk the road to which I have been called. But, I have met a lot of people in these early years. I have been privileged to travel all over the world and to interact with many different people.

I like to tell people that I'm something of a Christian schizophrenic. My earliest experiences of ministry were as a singer-songwriter. Just when I expected my music ministry to really take off, God called me to the pastorate in a local church. His leading was clear, so, instead of pursuing a promising career as a musician, Coletta and I moved to Cincinnati, Ohio where I became a youth pastor. That was 10 years ago. Just this past summer I resigned from my position as youth pastor in order to be available for some new ministry opportunities involving speaking and writing.

There have been other changes along the way, of course. Several years ago, God moved us to Colorado where I joined the staff of a young and growing church while I attended Denver Theological Seminary. Since graduation I have had the opportunity to speak around the country. I joined the faculty of Denver Seminary as an adjunct professor of theology. I'm

currently working on a Ph.D. in New Testament Studies at
Trinity College in Bristol, England. Recently, I've written for
Leadership Journal and just published a scholarly article on Old
Testament interpretation in the Biblical Theology Bulletin.

This brief biography of my life underscores the variety of
circles I've been privileged to move in over the past several
years. From biblical scholars to newly converted high school
students, I've had the opportunity to hear many people talk
about the gospel.

Very rarely in all these years, among all these different sorts
of people, have I heard an explanation of the gospel of Jesus
Christ that really encompasses that the Bible teaches about the
"good news." This is not to say that the gospel most Christians
proclaim today is wrong, just incomplete.

Select a random sampling of conservative Christians from
among a variety of backgrounds – Evangelical, Pentecostal,
mainline, Catholic, etc. – and ask them to describe the gospel.
You'll get a remarkably consistent answer. It will sound
something like this:

> The gospel is the good news that Jesus
> Christ, by his sacrificial death on the Cross
> and his Resurrection on the third day, has
> freed us from sin and death, allowing us to
> have eternal life with God in heaven.

Again, let me emphasize that there is nothing actually *false*
in such a definition. It's just not the full picture.

Once a year, Coletta and I visit something called the Parade
of Homes. This is an open-house event where custom home
builders and interior decorators get to show off their high-end
work. The houses are usually priced in the million-dollar range.
We love to look at the extravagant architecture. Sometimes, we

are so awe-struck just by the foyers in these homes that we almost forget to continue on and look at the rest of the house.

Our current preaching of the gospel is like this in some ways. Today's version of the gospel focuses on the forgiveness of sin. The good news, it says, is that sin no longer separates us from God. And certainly this is good news, but there's more to the gospel than just this. That is not quite what was in view when Jesus began going throughout the villages, "preaching the gospel" (Lk. 9:6).

The Gospel And The Kingdom

We should probably take a quick moment to explain what the word "gospel" means in a technical sense. Confusion exists because we sometimes talk about the "Gospel" of Matthew, Mark, Luke or John and yet we also say that someone is proclaiming the "gospel" without referring to those particular Bible books. The word "gospel" comes from the Greek *euangelion* refers to a "proclamation of good news." More often than not, a *euangelion* was a specific message announcing a military victory over enemy forces.

Why did Jesus choose this word to describe His message? Because at its heart, the gospel has more to do with the proclamation of a victory than it does with having our sins forgiven.

Most people I speak to are shocked to learn that the words "gospel" or "good news" and "forgiveness" never occur together in Scripture.

Never. Not one single time. And yet almost everyone defines the gospel as the good news of forgiveness. Everyone but Jesus, that is!

Again, the notion of the gospel as good news of forgiveness isn't wrong, but it's missing a very important element, an element which was absolutely central to Jesus' own teaching on the subject.   In most instances when Jesus used the term "gospel," the word was part of a larger phrase: "the gospel of the Kingdom." For instance:

> "The gospel of the kingdom shall be preached in the whole world as a testimony to all the nations..."
>
> (Matthew 24:14)

> "The Law and the Prophets were proclaimed until John; since that time the gospel of the kingdom of God has been preached..."
>
> (Luke 16:16)

So, while we usually define the gospel as the good news of forgiveness, Jesus defined it as the good news *of the Kingdom of God*. We must also remember, however, that his earliest listeners would have understood this to mean the *victory* of the Kingdom of God. We will explore this idea of the victory of the Kingdom more in a later chapter.

I have come to be profoundly convinced that the Kingdom of God is not simply an essential component of the gospel message according to Jesus, but is also a central theme of the entire Bible. But it is a theme which has, for one reason or another, been largely ignored in conservative Christian circles in the last few centuries. Over the years, our understanding of the gospel has veered at least slightly off course. This is especially true in the United States.

Of course, American Christianity is not necessarily indicative of Christian faith around the world. I know this should be obvious and I am delighted if you are rolling your eyes at this point and saying "duh!" But not everyone is.

When I began doctoral work in England, I made a rather surprising discovery: British Christians are different than American Christians. I'm not talking about their accents or their taste in food or anything like that. I'm referring to their understandings and orientations. British Christians tend to approach their faith from a different perspective.

Individualism And American Christianity

The primary context for American Christianity is individualism. We talk about what Jesus has done for *me*. We sing songs that are filled with statements like "*I* want to know you...*I* want to touch you." We define salvation as forgiveness of "*my* sins." We ask one another questions like "How is *your* walk with the Lord?" or "What has God been teaching *you* lately?"

Now, I'm not saying that any of this is wrong: After all, the Psalms are filled with very personal struggles and exaltations. When Peter was asked by the distraught crowd in Jerusalem what they needed to do to be saved, his answer targeted individuals: "Repent and be baptized, *each one of you,* in the name of Jesus for the remission of your sins" (Acts 2:38). I believe the phrase 'each one of you' was particularly significant for the Jewish crowd who largely expected God's favor to rest on them by virtue of the simple fact that they were descendents of His chosen people. "That's not enough," Peter said to them, "each one of you has to make the decision to repent of your sins and publicly confess your trust in Jesus Christ."

So, there's nothing inherently wrong with approaching the Christian faith as individuals; in fact, we can't avoid it. However, in America we are so steeped in individualism that it can distort our perspective. It is almost impossible for us to think about anything from any perspective but individualism.

We approach Christianity asking questions like, "What's in it for me?" or "What benefit will I receive if I do this or that?"

British Christianity is somewhat different. I may well be overstating the case, because I'm certainly no expert on English spirituality. I haven't made any exhaustive studies, but I have made some very interesting observations. British Christians can be individualistic as well, but their individualism seems to be tempered somewhat by a competing mind-set: that of citizens of a monarchy.

What I mean is, the British know what it means to live as citizens of a monarchy. Even in the present democratic context, the people retain a cultural memory of the monarchy that has defined British society for so long. The idea of being a subject of a kingdom, under the rule of a sovereign monarch, remains deeply ingrained in their social consciousness. This is difficult for Americans to grasp. We have no royal family. We elect the people who fill our highest political offices, which means that, in a very real sense, the true power belongs to us, not them. We are not *subjects* of our government and so certain aspects of the gospel of the Kingdom will be difficult for us to grasp. This is not necessarily the case for the British, however.

Now, this is not a book about politics or sociology, so I have no intention of unpacking what I realize is a broad and sweeping generalization. All I want to do is make a simple point: the British seem to be more attuned to issues of kings and kingdoms. They know what it means to be the subject of a monarch. I believe this to be true because one of the first things I noticed as I began to interact with British Christians is that the Kingdom is more important to the British than it is to most American Christians.

I don't mean simply that they talk about it more often. After all, Americans talk about doing "Kingdom work" and "expanding the Kingdom" and things like that as well. But for Americans, Kingdom-talk is often vague...as though it's language we employ only out of respect for long-lost tradition. But for the British, the days of their political monarchy are not so thoroughly shrouded in the fog of history. They still have a royal family! And so, their Christian Kingdom-talk is not only more frequent, but more profound as well.

When I first noticed this, I was mildly intrigued. The more I listened to it, however, the more I became convinced that Americans are missing out on something profoundly important simply because our culture has conditioned us to think in terms that make Kingdom-talk hard to grasp.

We've never had a king. We've never been subjects of a kingdom. But Christians, the Bible says, *do* have a king and *are* subjects of His kingdom. How can we, as Americans, grasp such truth?

The fact is, we're not quite sure. Answering that question requires that we orient our thinking in an unfamiliar direction. That is what the rest this book is about.

This is the *Kingdom for the* – formerly – *kingless.*

THREE

Kingdom-Talk

It is interesting to note that the actual phrase "Kingdom of God" is not used in the Old Testament. At first glance, this is somewhat puzzling, since it is used so frequently in the New Testament.

In the New Testament, the precise phrase, "Kingdom of God" occurs 66 times, usually from Jesus himself:

> But when Jesus saw this, He was indignant and said to them, "Permit the children to come to Me; do not hinder them; for the kingdom of God belongs to such as these."
>
> (Mark 10:13)

The Kingdom Of *Heaven*

Other references to this divine Kingdom take slightly different form. For some reason, Matthew seems to have generally preferred the phrase "Kingdom of Heaven." Why this is so is not entirely clear and is, in fact, the matter of some scholarly debate. I, personally, am inclined to think that Matthew was following Jewish tradition and was simply hesitant to invoke names for God out of respect for Him. Even today, Jewish people will often go out of their way to avoid unnecessary invocation of God's name. Just recently, I was reading an editorial by a Jewish Rabbi who notated God this way: G-d. For many conservative Jewish people, casual invocation of God's name was disrespectful and so to be avoided. I suspect that something similar motivated Matthew to render most references to the Kingdom of God as "Kingdom of Heaven." On the four occasions when he did use the more common New Testament phrase, he seems to have done so for dramatic purposes (cf. Matthew 12:28, 19:24, 21:31 and 21:43).

In any event, Matthew's "Kingdom of Heaven"[6] phrase gives every appearance of functioning as a synonym of the more common "Kingdom of God":

> And Jesus said to His disciples, "Truly I say to you, it is hard for a rich man to enter the kingdom of heaven. Again I say to you, it is easier for a camel to go through the eye of a needle, than for a rich man to enter the kingdom of God."
>
> (Matthew 19:23-24)

Here, in a manner that is typical of Hebrew rhetoric, Jesus makes the same point twice, with the second involving a slight intensification of the message: *it is hard, harder in fact, than for a camel to go through the eye of the needle, for a rich man to enter the Kingdom of God*[7]. Note that the Kingdom of God phrase occurs in the second half of this construction, perhaps indicating a slight intensification of the more generic Kingdom of Heaven. In any event, the generally synonymous meaning of the two phrases is clear.

---

[6] Or, literally, "Kingdom of the Heavens"

[7] What makes it difficult is not the wealth, per-se, but the tendency to place trust in wealth to such an extent that the rich are often unable to trust in anything else, including Jesus.

Other References To The Kingdom

Numerous other references to this Kingdom are found throughout the New Testament, but signaled by other constructions:

> Jesus was going throughout all Galilee, teaching in their synagogues and proclaiming the gospel of *the kingdom*, and healing every kind of disease and every kind of sickness among the people.
>
> (Matthew 4:23)

> "You are those who have stood by Me in My trials; and just as My Father has granted Me a kingdom, I grant you that you may eat and drink at My table in *My kingdom*, and you will sit on thrones judging the twelve tribes of Israel."
>
> (Luke 22:28-30)

> Therefore, brethren, be all the more diligent to make certain about His calling and choosing you; for as long as you practice these things, you will never stumble; for in this way the entrance into *the eternal kingdom* of our Lord and Savior Jesus Christ will be abundantly supplied to you.
>
> (2 Peter 1:10-11)

Similar references to God's Kingdom are found in the Old Testament as well:

> Your throne, O God, is forever and ever; a
> scepter of uprightness is the scepter of *Your*
> *kingdom.*
>
> (Psalm 45:6)

> "In the days of those kings the God of heaven
> will set up *a kingdom* which will never be
> destroyed, and *that kingdom* will not be left for
> another people; it will crush and put an end to
> all these kingdoms, but it will itself endure
> forever."
>
> (Daniel 2:44)

All Nations, Under God

By far the most common use of the word kingdom in the
Old Testament, however, is in reference to *human kingdoms.* In
this sense, the word kingdom in the Old Testament is essentially
equivalent to a *political nation* and the most important nation in
the Old Testament is, of course, Israel. Even here, though, the
use of the word kingdom is not entirely secular, for God plays a
major role in Israel's politics. In fact, human kings of Israel are
often portrayed as operating more as regents of God's authority
than as genuinely sovereign rulers:

> Samuel said to Saul, "You have acted foolishly;
> you have not kept the commandment of the
> LORD your God, which He commanded you,
> for now the LORD would have established your
> kingdom over Israel forever."
>
> (1 Samuel 13:13)

> He said to Jeroboam, "Take for yourself ten
> pieces; for thus says the LORD, the God of
> Israel, 'Behold, I will tear the kingdom out of
> the hand of Solomon and give you ten tribes'"
>
> (1 Kings 11:31)

In regard to Israel this is not, in and of itself, a very surprising notion. On the contrary, this is quite in keeping with the typical Ancient Near Eastern worldview, which held that each nation had a patron god or goddess. In this conception of reality, each nation was thought to be a sort of tool by which the various deities carried out their wills. Perhaps you've seen old movies based on Greek mythology. These movies often show gods and goddesses playing a game of chess, where each move on the game board results in certain events happening in the real world. Or, if that doesn't work for you, think of the original Star Wars movie. In one scene of that film, Chewbacca and R2D2 are playing a game that looks a lot like chess, except that the pieces are holographic creatures that do the bidding of the game players. This is very much the way people in the Ancient Near East thought about gods and nations as players and pawns. So, the conception of God as being able to raise up and cast down Israelite kings is not surprising at all.

What *is* surprising, however, is the fact that God is also portrayed as having this kind of authority over *other* nations:

> (Daniel, speaking to the Babylonian king
> Nebuchadnezzer): "You, O king, are the king of
> kings, to whom the God of heaven has given the
> kingdom, the power, the strength and the glory;"
>
> (Daniel 2:37)

(Daniel, speaking to the Babylonian King
Belshazzar): "Now this is the inscription that
was written out: 'MENE, MENE, TEKEL,
UPHARSIN.' This is the interpretation of the
message: 'MENE' -- God has numbered your
kingdom and put an end to it. 'TEKEL' -- you
have been weighed on the scales and found
deficient. 'PERES' -- your kingdom has been
divided and given over to the Medes and
Persians."

(Daniel 5:25-28)

...and he said, "O LORD, the God of our
fathers, are You not God in the heavens? And
are You not ruler over all the kingdoms of the
nations? Power and might are in Your hand so
that no one can stand against You."

(2 Chronicles 20:6)

To 21st century believers, the idea of God having ultimate
authority over all nations is perfectly natural. It would only be
unnatural to think otherwise. But, we have to realize how
utterly foreign such a concept was to the people of that time
period.

But so what? What significance is there in the fact that God
claimed ultimate authority over all kingdoms and not just over
Israel? The significance of this fact lies in what it does to our
understanding of God's special relationship to the nation or
kingdom of Israel. For, while it is true that God is sovereign
over all nations, it is also true, and extremely significant, that
He is called the God of Israel as happens literally hundreds of
times in the Old Testament. He has sovereignty over all the
other nations, but He is never called the God *of* them.

The Special Significance of Israel[8]

What does this mean? While all nations were under God's control, only Israel was intended to be *the visible manifestation of God's sovereign rule.*

There are certainly many different ways to think about kingdoms, but on one fundamental level, kingdoms are simply manifestations of a ruler's power; that is, a kingdom is simply that place where a king's rule and reign is greatest. Any genuine king has power that extends beyond the borders of his country. Unless he is a very weak king, he is able to exert some degree of military force or trade pressure or do any number of other things that force other nations to take him seriously. Of course, his power is limited somewhat outside his own kingdom, but it exists nonetheless. A king's kingdom, then, is that place where his rule and reign are greatest.

God's sovereign power was not lessened outside of Israel, of course. The very notion is absurd since, as an omnipotent King, His power could never decrease in any way. Geography and political boundaries are absolutely irrelevant to God's reign. However, while His control cannot be lessened, it can be less visible in some places than in others. This is what I mean when I say that Israel was the visible manifestation of God's rule and reign.

Why would God choose to limit the manifestation of His rule and reign over human affairs to a particular nation? We cannot say for sure, but I think we can make a fairly intelligent guess.

---

[8] This is an extremely brief treatment of this complex topic. For more detail, I refer the reader to this excellent work: Brent Kinman, *History, Design And The End of Time* (Nashville: Broadman & Holman Publishers, 2000), 29-48 and 91-103.

The other day, I was playing outside with my daughters. It was snowing, the kind of thick, fluffy flakes that you only find in Colorado in the early spring. When we first went outside, we were extremely aware of the flakes; brushing them off our hair, catching them on our tongues. After a while, though, we stopped paying attention to them. In fact, I became entirely unaware of the falling snow until an evergreen branch dumped its cache of the stuff down my collar.

I think God's decision to visibly manifest His reign in the lives of one group of people was motivated by His desire to make all people sit up and take notice. That was the purpose of the kingdom of Israel.

As such, the kingdom of Israel can be said to be one manifestation of the Kingdom of God. If this seems too abstract, think about it this way: the nation of Israel was the earthly illustration of a spiritual reality, the sovereign authority of God over human affairs.

The Kingdom of God itself is the rule and reign of God over human history. Obviously, God always reigns over human life, but as with a human kingdom, God's rule and reign can be manifested in different ways at different times and this is precisely what He has done.

In the Old Testament period, the primary manifestation of God's Kingdom was the nation of Israel, but in the first century A.D., God began to manifest this rule and reign in a startlingly different way: through the person of Jesus Christ.

Once attuned to Kingdom-talk, it becomes difficult to miss the centrality of this message in Jesus' ministry. As we have already noted, most of the occurrences of the phrase "Kingdom of God" in the New Testament come from Jesus Himself. John the Baptist used the phrase[9] at least once in his ministry of announcing the arrival of Jesus (Mat. 3:2), but apart from this,

---

[9] Or, more precisely, the Matthean equivalent: "Kingdom of Heaven."

almost all of the occurrences of the phrase in the Gospels come from Jesus' lips.

There are at least three important aspects of Jesus' Kingdom-talk of which we must make note if we are to understand what he meant by such language. As Jesus taught about the Kingdom of God, he seemed to envision it as something that could be possessed, entered, and/or experienced.

"Possessing" The Kingdom

By *possessed*, I mean simply that Jesus often likened the Kingdom of God to something that we could have, like a treasure. It was in this sense that he described the Kingdom of God as something which could be taken away from one group of people (Israel) and given to another:

> "Therefore I say to you, the kingdom of God will be taken away from you and given to a people, producing the fruit of it."
>
> (Matthew 21:43)

Jesus also implied this meaning when he compared the Kingdom to something so valuable that wise people would go to extraordinary lengths to attain it, such as a treasure or pearl (Mat. 13:44-46).

Now, if the Kingdom of God is, most literally, the rule and reign of God in human affairs, then how can anyone be said to possess it? This may seem confusing at first, but it becomes less so when we remember that such statements are metaphorical. We humans cannot, of course, own the Kingdom as we would own a piece of gold or a brilliant pearl, but metaphors do not depend on one thing being exactly like another, only on there being at least one point of genuine similarity.

If you think of refugees who will go to almost any lengths to come to America, you may begin to understand something of what Jesus is describing when he talks of the Kingdom this way.

I have a friend whose family came to the United States from Vietnam. His story of their journey is nothing short of astounding. While his mother was still pregnant with him, my friend's father, mother and sister loaded into a boat not much larger than a bathtub, powered by an engine built from lawnmower parts. They traveled down a river and out into the China Sea. After days adrift in rough waters, they somehow landed on the coast of Malaysia where my friend was born on the beach. Eventually, a benevolent sponsor made it possible for them to all come to the United States.

Why would they go through all that? Because, at least to them, America represented more than a geographic location or a particular political system. It represented freedom and opportunities that just weren't possible in their homeland. And so does the Kingdom of God. We cannot, of course, own the Kingdom, but we can possess it in a way by putting ourselves in a position to be able to take advantage of all it offers. In that sense, the Kingdom, and all it has to offer, is *ours*.

"Entering" The Kingdom

Jesus also speaks of the kingdom as something that can be *entered*. In many of his teachings, the Kingdom sounds very much like a particular place. In this sense, Jesus spoke of particular kinds of people as being inside or outside the Kingdom:

"Truly I say to you that the tax collectors and
prostitutes will get into the kingdom of God
before you." (speaking to some Jewish leaders
who opposed him)

(Matthew 21:31)

"Truly I say to you, whoever does not receive
the kingdom of God like a child will not enter it
at all."

(Luke 18:17)

Talking about the Kingdom as a place seems to
communicate the ideas of inclusion and exclusion; that is, that
some people are inside the Kingdom and some people are
outside of it.

As Jesus speaks of the Kingdom in such terms, one of the
surprising things to note is the kind of people that he includes as
being on the inside: prostitutes, tax collectors, and sinners. Of
course, among such people, the ones Jesus describes as being in
the Kingdom are those who have repented and turned from their
ways. So perhaps we should better describe them as *former*
prostitutes, tax collectors and slaves. Still, the inclusion of such
people was a very difficult idea for many of Jesus' original
listeners to accept. But Jesus had even more shocking things to
say about those who would and would not get into the
Kingdom.

In the eighth chapter of Matthew, we find a very interesting
parable Jesus told. It was occasioned by a conversation with a
Roman centurion, a gentile, who had responded to Jesus in such
a way that Jesus exclaimed, "Truly I say to you, I have not
found such great faith with anyone in Israel!" Moreover, he
went on to say that, in the end, many people would enter the
Kingdom of Heaven from all nations on earth while the "sons of

the kingdom" would be cast into outer darkness where there would be "weeping and gnashing of teeth" (Mat. 8:12). As shocking as it may sound – and certainly it was more shocking to Jesus' original audience than to us – I take these "sons of the kingdom" who were cast out into eternal darkness to be the unbelieving Israelites.

All Israelites were, in one sense, "sons of the Kingdom" simply by virtue of the fact that they were born into the nation in which God had chosen to manifest His rule and reign. However, what Jesus proclaimed here and at other times, was that belonging to the nation that was the *manifestation* of God's Kingdom did not automatically qualify one for citizenship in the heavenly Kingdom itself. This latter, and far more important, citizenship was conferred by faith and not by ancestry.

"Experiencing" The Kingdom

Perhaps the most significant aspect of Jesus' Kingdom-talk, however, was his description of the Kingdom as something that could be *experienced*. I consider this the most significant aspect simply because it is the one for which all of us most long. We desire to know that God is near to us, that He is active in our lives. We want to know God *Himself*, and not just facts *about* Him[10]. When we serve Him, we want desperately to know that He is working through us and that our labor is not in vain. In short, we want to experience Him, and this is precisely what this aspect of Kingdom-talk promises.

---

[10] Although I must add that you cannot truly know God without knowing facts about Him as well. If I could not tell you the color of my wife's eyes or her favorite foods or where she was born or what she likes to do for fun…you would probably question whether or not I really knew her at all. It is true that you can know about someone without knowing them personally, but the converse is not true: you cannot know someone personally without knowing certain things about them.

A great many of the references in the Gospels to the Kingdom of God are connected with signs and wonders. On many instances Jesus pointed to his miracles as evidence of the arrival of the Kingdom. At one point, John the Baptist sent men to ask Jesus, "Are you the expected one or should we look for someone else?" Interestingly, Jesus did not immediately answer the question. Instead, he began healing people. Then, turning back to John's disciples, he said to them, "Go, report to John what you have seen and heard." The miracles themselves were the answer to John's question and they spoke louder than any affirmative words.

All of the Gospel writers seem to have understood this connection between signs and wonders and the Kingdom, for we are told on numerous occasions that Jesus went around preaching about the Kingdom *and* performing miracles:

> Jesus was going throughout all Galilee, teaching in their synagogues and proclaiming the gospel of the kingdom, and healing every kind of disease and every kind of sickness among the people.
>
> (Matthew 4:23)

Even more interesting are those places in the Gospel accounts when Jesus sent out disciples. In such cases, he apparently delegated his power to his followers and told them to use it as a means of proving the truth of the proclamation they were to make:

> And He called the twelve together, and gave them power and authority over all the demons and to heal diseases. And He sent them out to proclaim the kingdom of God and to perform

> healing. And He said to them, "Take nothing for your journey, neither a staff, nor a bag, nor bread, nor money; and do not even have two tunics apiece. Whatever house you enter, stay there until you leave that city. And as for those who do not receive you, as you go out from that city, shake the dust off your feet as a testimony against them." Departing, they began going throughout the villages, preaching the gospel and healing everywhere.
>
> (Luke 9:1-6)

As we see in the above passage, these miraculous signs included not only healings but also the casting out of demons. In our modern culture, the very idea of demonic spirits is a bit hard to swallow. For those outside the church, belief in demons is tantamount to belief in the Tooth Fairy and the Easter Bunny. Even inside the church, the belief in demons is generally a "back burner" belief at best. In part, this is because certain groups of Christians have over-emphasized the involvement of demonic spirits in the world, seeing demons behind just about everything bad that happens. Reacting to this, and to the world's general skepticism about demonic spirits, the evangelical church has often under-emphasized the role of demons in the world today.

Demons are not all-powerful nor are they all-present. Not everything bad that happens is because of their involvement. However, the fact remains that they *do* exist and that they *are* involved in the world around us. The Gospels have a surprisingly great interest in this fact, probably because Jesus himself did as well. Like the miracles of healing, demonic exorcism played a central role in Jesus' announcement of the Kingdom of God and Jesus went out of his way to make this connection explicit:

"...if I cast out demons by the Spirit of God, then the kingdom of God has come upon you."
(Matthew 12:28)

Whether by healing the lame, curing the sick or casting out demons, these miraculous events all point to the Kingdom of God. That is why they are often called "signs," because they are announcements of the presence of the Kingdom. If the Kingdom of God is the rule and reign of God Himself, then we ought to expect His power to be visibly present wherever His reign is being manifested.

Jesus' interactions with demonic spirits also point to another aspect of the Kingdom. We will save the details for another chapter, but the basic fact is worth noting here: in addition to the Kingdom of God, the Bible also has a great deal to say about the kingdom of *darkness*. In many ways, the announcement of the coming of the Kingdom of God is also an announcement of victory over this evil kingdom, which has long had such power in the world. In fact, it is arguable that the choice of the Greek word *euangelion*[11], which we translate as "gospel" was specifically intended to communicate this very thing.

So, in addition to being something we can possess and enter into, the Kingdom of God is often described as being something we can experience. We experience the Kingdom by experiencing the power of its King. Or at least the Bible seems to indicate that we *should*. In practice, much of the Church seems to be failing to experience such power. Divorce, drug and alcohol problems, addictions to pornography, and a host of other infirmities are just as much a part of the Church as they

---

[11] And which, you may recall, often refers to the announcement of a military victory.

are of the world. And this power-shortage does not just manifest itself in sin. Our worship is often lackluster; our service and outreach mediocre at best. If the Church is the manifestation of the Kingdom of God, then where is the power of her King? I believe much of the problem rests in the fact that we have not made room in our lives and in our churches for the working of a King whose Kingdom we have so radically failed to understand.

Simply understanding the different ways in which the Bible speaks of the Kingdom will not remedy this situation, but it is a start.

Jesus And The Kingdom

Now, none of the types of Kingdom-talk mentioned above would have been difficult for the average first-century Jewish person to understand. In fact, they would probably have already thought of the Kingdom of God in these sorts of terms. What was surprising, however, was the fact that Jesus added two new elements to his Kingdom-talk.

The first of these was the idea that the Kingdom of God was his…that he had ownership of it:

> "You are those who have stood by Me in My trials; and just as My Father has granted Me a kingdom, I grant you that you may eat and drink at My table in My kingdom, and you will sit on thrones judging the twelve tribes of Israel."
>
> (Luke 22:30)

> Jesus answered, "My kingdom is not of this world. If My kingdom were of this world, then My servants would be fighting so that I would

not be handed over to the Jews; but as it is, My
kingdom is not of this realm."

(John 18:36)

It is probably not possible for us, as modern readers, to understand how radical a thing it was for Jesus to make such claims. If you look carefully at the two preceding verse, you will notice that he claims three things: royal authority in general, royal authority over Israel particularly and royal authority that is "not of this world"; that is, royal authority that is spiritual in nature.

By such claims, Jesus asserted both his role as Messiah and his divine nature. Make no mistake about it, these were the kinds of claims that led to the cross.

Recently, I was asked to participate in a panel discussion regarding Mel Gibson's film, "The Passion of the Christ." The event was intended as an outreach opportunity by the church that sponsored it. In the interest of fair discussion, other members of the panel included a Catholic priest, a Jewish rabbi and an agnostic. Much of the evening's discussion centered around the question "Who was responsible for Jesus' crucifixion?"

Various answers were given. The rabbi felt the movie blamed the Jewish people. The agnostic thought it was human violence in general (assuming that the event actually happened, of which he wasn't really convinced). The priest presented a very good argument that it made more sense to speak of all of our sins as being responsible for Jesus' death. Now, certainly, I agreed with the priest's answer in many ways, but when it was my turn to answer, I said that it was really Jesus who was responsible for Jesus' death. After all, I argued, the Torah prescribed death for anyone found guilty of blasphemy. To blaspheme essentially means to slander God, but one way to do that was to claim for yourself prerogatives that belong only to God. And this is precisely what Jesus did: he accepted worship, reinterpreted the Sabbath law, forgave sins and, as we've just seen, spoke of God's Kingdom as being his. Such claims are blasphemous because by them, Jesus claimed to be God. From the Jewish perspective, Jesus' accusers were right...at least they would have been if they hadn't been so wrong.

What I mean is, if any mere man had claimed what Jesus claimed, then the cross would have been a fit punishment. But Jesus was no mere man. His claim to divine prerogatives was justified because he was God. The mistake of the Jewish leaders was not in missing the significance of Jesus' claims, but in *failing to recognize the truth of them*. If you didn't believe that Jesus was who he claimed to be, executing him as a blasphemer made perfect sense. By his claims, Jesus forced his accusers against the wall: either accept me for who I claim to be or execute me. Since their hardened hearts kept them from doing the former, the latter was their only choice. In that sense, it was Jesus himself who was responsible for the cross.

Certainly the idea that Jesus was God incarnate, and therefore that the Kingdom of God was his, was a shocking enough claim for the Jewish people of Jesus' day. However, Jesus made another claim that was, if possible, even more shocking: he claimed that the Kingdom would be taken away from the Jewish people.

We have already seen this claim above in the verses we looked at while exploring the idea of the Kingdom as something that could be given or taken, but they are important enough to bear repeating:

> "Therefore I say to you, the kingdom of God
> will be taken away from you and given to a
> people, producing the fruit of it."

(Matthew 21:43)

This promise, or curse, is made explicit only here in Matthew 21:43, though other biblical texts seem to address the same issue (cf. Mat. 3:9, Lk. 3:8, et al). Jesus' words here are the subject of much scholarly debate, because they have profound implications for the way we understand present-day Israel and the status of the Jews as the Chosen People of God.

If you hold that Jews remain the Chosen People, you have two possible responses to Matthew 21:43. First, you may argue that the curse is not against the Jewish people generally, but only against the Jewish leadership which opposed Jesus. This makes some sense in the context in which the statement was made, but the "people" to whom the Kingdom will be given are likely gentiles. This is clearly implied by the use of the Greek *ethnos* which the Jews of Jesus' day used to refer to all non-Jewish people. If Jesus had meant to say that the Kingdom would be taken away from certain Jewish leaders and given to other Jewish people, there are other words he could have used[12]. Another option is to argue that this was not a prophetic statement but only a *hypothetical* threat; that is, that Jesus never intended to actually take the Kingdom away, but was only saying this as a way of rebuking the Jewish people and bringing them back in line with God's will. The difficulty with this approach is that, as the New Testament clearly shows, the Kingdom does seem to have passed to the gentiles, at least for the present time.

The fact is that the question of the role of national Israel in God's continuing plan of redemption is extremely complicated. If anything, this is probably a ridiculous understatement. Many books have been written exploring that question alone and we

---

[12] The most likely choice would have been the word *laos* which was often used to refer to Jewish people in general.

certainly do not have time to review all the arguments and evidences here.

Don't misunderstand me: the question is important. We just don't have time to explore it in any depth here. This was supposed to be a very short book and it is already longer than I intended it to be. So, in the interest of both brevity and intellectual integrity, which is not fostered by a toe-dip in deep waters, we're going to lay the question aside for now.

We do need to acknowledge, however, at least one thing which I hope will not engender too much debate: at present, neither Israel nor the Jewish people are the primary means by which God manifests His rule and reign in human affairs. Instead, it is the Church which is the present visible manifestation of the Kingdom of God. Saying as much does not necessarily exclude national Israel from having any role currently, nor does it necessarily presume anything about what things might look like at some future stage of history.

Of course, the Church is not exactly a simple matter. Confusion abounds on this subject and it is necessary even to define what we mean by the "Church."

The Church Is An Organism

For some people, the word "Church" means the Catholic Church. For others, the Church is a building, as in "I go to that church on the corner there." Hang around Christians long enough and you are likely to hear talk of a visible and an invisible Church, local churches and a universal Church. But what is the Church?

There is no simple answer to that. Sometimes, in an attempt to cut through the confusion, Christians will say that the Church is people; specifically, it is the people of God, defined as that body of individuals who have trusted in Jesus. Of course, defining the Church this way just begs other questions, for this is the definition of Israel as well. In fact, that's the literal meaning of the word "Israel" – God's people.

Still, leaving other questions aside for a bit, in many ways, this is a fine definition of the Church. The Church is, after all, made up of people. In fact, the very word for the Church in the original Greek of the New Testament was *ekklasia* which literally means an *assembly or gathering of people.* In this sense, the Church is a group of people who have been called together out of the world. This is fine as far as it goes, but things grow more complicated when we look at the larger witness of Scripture.

The Church Is An Organization

The definition of the Church as people is often motivated by the desire to avoid confusing the true Church of God with some particular institution. This is understandable, but it is not so easily accomplished. Whether we like it or not, institutions come with the territory. Unfortunately, there seems to be a growing number of people today who claim the mantle of Christianity but who spurn the organized Church. Many of them have had bad experiences with organized Christianity and I feel a great deal of sympathy for them in this respect. The Church, tragically, can be a very dangerous place. However, I cannot condone their withdrawal from all forms of organized Christianity. To do so flies in the face of Jesus' clear instruction and sounds more like Eastern mysticism than Christian faith and practice.

Now, I'm not suggesting that every Christian needs to be part of a *particular* Christian institution. I'm not advocating one denomination over another or favoring large churches over small ones. I'm simply saying that the meeting together of Christians, guided by biblical commands regarding organization and practice, is not optional. Institutions are simply part of the package.

That's the way God intended it. God's rules for the Church include not only instructions for godly living, but also instructions for Church offices (such as elders and deacons), observances (baptism and communion) and finances. These things all imply an institutional dimension to the Church. So, as true as it is that the Church is primarily people, we have to acknowledge that it is not *only* people; there's more to it than that.

The Church is both an *organism* and an *organization*. As an organism, it is composed of living cells (believers). As an organization, it is a visible social institution marked by rules of conduct, government, financial transactions, physical buildings, etc.

The Wheat From The Chaff

If we think about the Church in these terms, however, a serious problem arises: the Church-as-organization may not always be perfectly synonymous with the Church-as-organism. Look at any given local church on a typical Sunday morning. At least a few of the people attending worship services are probably not genuine believers. At the very least, there will probably be some children attending who have not yet come to faith. As a former youth pastor, I can attest that there will probably also be some teenagers who have not decided to follow Jesus, and who are not in church by choice. There may be unbelieving husbands or wives who come with their believing spouses just to keep the peace. There may even be individuals who grew up in the Church and consider themselves Christian, but who have never actually submitted themselves to saving faith in Jesus Christ.

This sort of hodge-podge of believers and unbelievers is implied by many of the parables Jesus taught. Jesus often described the Kingdom by means of parables that involved a final act of separating the true from the untrue: good fish from bad fish, sheep from goats, wheat from tares, etc. He also spoke of the Kingdom as a wedding feast in which certain guests were dismissed from the celebration because they were not properly attired. Perhaps you remember it. In this parable, Jesus described a king who threw a wedding feast for his son. When the invited guests not only refused to come, but even slaughtered the king's messengers, the king invited people in from the streets. Among this group, however, one was found unworthy of being present at the feast:

> "But when the king came in to look over the dinner guests, he saw a man there who was not dressed in wedding clothes, and he said to him, 'Friend, how did you come in here without wedding clothes?' And the man was speechless. Then the king said to the servants, 'Bind him hand and foot, and throw him into the outer darkness; in that place there will be weeping and gnashing of teeth.'"
>
> (Matthew 22:11-13)

This parable seems to have two parts. First, the parable appears to be an indication of God's frustration with national Israel. Not only had the nation repeatedly refused God's entreaties, but they had killed His prophets and messengers. The second part of this parable, however, I take as referring to the Church. The primary manifestation of the Kingdom has passed from Israel to the Church, but this fact does not mean that everyone who associates with a church will be saved in the end. It is association with Jesus, not just with the institution through which his Kingdom is manifest, that matters in the end. On several occasions, Jesus declared that many who had thought themselves his followers by virtue of their earthly associations would be told in the end: *Away from me. I never knew you.*

So, it seems clear that any given local church may contain unbelievers. Some will be aware of their status as such and some may have deluded themselves into thinking otherwise, but their presence remains a fact. So how should we think about them?

Some Christians will argue that such individuals are not really part of the true Church, but only part of a particular local church; and, what's more, it's not fair to even think of them as truly being part of the local church. This is only the perception of outsiders. That is why we must speak of the visible and the invisible church.

But if we take this approach, then we have to apply the same principle on a larger scale. Some whole churches may be apostate, disregarding basic teachings of Christianity. Some churches may allow non-believers to belong, include them on the membership rosters and allow, even encourage, them to take part in communion. Some churches may even allow people living in clear disregard of the teachings of Scripture to be leaders; pastors, elders and teachers.

For these reasons, we really have no choice but to make the distinction between the universal Church and specific local churches which may or may not belong to the larger entity; between the visible church which is comprised of both believers and unbelievers and the invisible Church, which consists only of believers but is ultimately discernable only by God and not by the watching world.

These divisions are troubling in some ways, because they make the definition of the Church ambiguous. It would be much nicer if we could give a clear definition of the church that eliminated the need for what feels like some hedging of the bets. At the present time, however, that seems impossible.

The Church And Israel

We will do well to remember that we have precisely the same difficulty defining the Church as we do defining Israel. Israel, too, was both an organism and an organization. It had in its midst both believers and unbelievers. There were factions of it that went apostate and factions that remained obedient. And, of course, most importantly, Israel exists as a nation for the express purpose of demonstrating the reign of God, of the Kingdom.

One of the key questions asked frequently when discussing both Israel and the Church is this: what is the relationship between the two?   Are the Church and Israel the same thing? Has the Church replaced Israel?

This will hardly be a sufficient answer to these, and other, difficult questions, but one way to think about the subject is like this: the greatest common denominator between both Israel and the Church, is their status as manifestations of the Kingdom of God. Both Israel and the Church are intended primarily to show the world the reality of God's rule and reign.   They are announcements intended to give the world an opportunity to respond to the one true King. It is God's *use* of the two groups which makes them what they are.   They do not define themselves.

Think of God's reign as *rain*: it pours out on a particular group of people at a particular time, drenching them and thus marking them visibly. At different times, the rain may pour out on different groups of people. However, because it is the same rain, different groups that it drenches will naturally have certain similarities, but they need not be perfectly synonymous, nor do all the people marked by the rain necessarily all have an equal share in the blessings of God; namely, salvation. Some are merely spattered while others, by faith, choose to seek the heaviest part of the downpour and be drenched to the soul. The Scripture is clear that it is faith which defines the true – shall we call them *spiritual* – people of God over and against those who have a mere institutional affiliation with the group through which His Kingdom is being manifest:

> ...so Abraham BELIEVED GOD, AND IT WAS RECKONED TO HIM AS RIGHTEOUSNESS. Therefore, be sure that it is those who are of faith who are sons of Abraham. The Scripture, foreseeing that God would justify the Gentiles by faith, preached the gospel beforehand to Abraham, saying, "ALL THE NATIONS WILL BE BLESSED IN YOU." So then those who are of faith are blessed with Abraham, the believer.
>
> (Galatians 3:6-9)

Israel and the church are not the same thing. There are certainly important differences: the Church is omni-ethnic and is not a political entity in the same way national Israel was. More importantly, certain descriptions of the Church are given that have no real parallel to Israel in the Old Testament period; particularly the description of the Church as the body of Christ, the "fullness of him who fills all in all" (Eph. 1:23)[13]. So, certainly, Israel and the Church are different, but at the same time, they are not *completely* different. They are distinct

---

[13]   Although I take this to be referring to that universal, invisible Church which is composed of true believers, be they Jewish or Gentile.

entities with much in common and their most important commonality is this: both are means by which the Kingdom of God has been made manifest. There are still important questions about Israel and the Church which can, and should, be asked and answered, but I will leave these to more able scholars. For now, I simply wish to drive home this simple point: the most important issue is the Kingdom itself and not the different signposts pointing to it. Both the Church and Israel are manifestations of the Kingdom.

Conclusion

All of the Bible's Kingdom-talk points to one central idea: The Kingdom of God itself is best understood as God's reign *over* and *in* human history.   God's sovereignty over human history never changes. How God manifests that reign in human history may vary from time to time and place to place. .

FOUR

In The King's Image

Coletta and I first met through Campus Crusade for Christ at Kent State University. One of the things that drew us together was a love for music and we first served together on the worship team for the weekly meetings.

We both played guitar, but we had learned it in very different ways. After a few years of teaching myself guitar, I had studied with a professional teacher for a while. He had been very helpful, particularly in helping to break me of some bad habits I had picked up. Coletta learned guitar from a friend who hadn't been playing for all that long herself. Unfortunately, while this friend taught her the basics, she also passed along some bad habits.

By the time Coletta and I started playing together, these habits were deeply ingrained in her playing style. They proved very hard to unlearn and this has always deeply hampered her technical development.

In the same way that bad technical habits impede the development of skills, misunderstandings are often a significant obstacle to real learning. Learning is never just the acquisition of new information. We are not blank slates. Everything we learn either adds to what we already know and believe or it replaces it. Sometimes, truth is rejected because it doesn't fit with our already-established ways of thinking.

Sometimes, developing a correct understanding of something can only be achieved after first demolishing our *misunderstandings* of it.

This is certainly the case when it comes to what it means to be made in the Image of God. The idea of humans having been made in God's Image looms large on the average Christian's mental landscape, but it is often a façade, a massive but ultimately paper-thin edifice resting on an insignificant foundation. We have heard it often enough, but what do these words from the very first chapter of Genesis mean?

> Then God said, "Let Us make man in Our image, according to Our likeness; and let them rule over the fish of the sea and over the birds of the sky and over the cattle and over all the earth, and over every creeping thing that creeps on the earth." God created man in His own image, in the image of God He created him; male and female He created them. God blessed them; and God said to them, "Be fruitful and multiply, and fill the earth, and subdue it; and rule over the fish of the sea and over the birds of the sky and over every living thing that moves on the earth."
>
> (Genesis 1:26-28)

The first chapter of Genesis has been the source of a great deal of debate in evangelical Christianity. Most of the debate centers around questions of how long ago the Creation took place and how long each of the "days" lasted. These are important questions, but I believe such debates have overshadowed the more central purpose of Genesis. There are actually two truths that Genesis 1 has been composed to communicate to us. First, God is the sovereign King. Second, human beings are His representatives.

It is always interesting to see the reactions to this article. Most people are immediately hostile skeptics. They don't believe it. They have all sorts of reasons why the study was probably flawed. Even those who aren't obviously hostile to the idea are generally uncomfortable with it.

Why these reactions? Because most people hold to the structuralist view. The idea that animals may possess the same abilities that we do threatens our view of our own uniqueness. Only human beings are made in the Image of God, therefore only human beings can possess these attributes.

Of course, we can always argue either that only humans possess the *entire set* of attributes or, that only humans have them to the *extent* that we do. But do we really want to suggest that humans are made in the Image of God only by virtue of the greater *degree* to which we possess a particular set of attributes? Surely not.

Now, this is primarily a theoretical difficulty. It is difficult to settle the question of whether or not certain animals really possess any or all of these abilities.

However, let me say one word that will clearly show that the structural view isn't out of the woods yet: *angels*. One has only to look to angels to find that the difficulty we're talking about here is not entirely theoretical. To the best of my knowledge, angels – and presumably demons as well – possess each and every attribute that is thought to constitute the Image of God in humans. It might even be argued that they not only possess them all, but, in some instances, possess them *to a greater degree than we do*. And yet, angels are never described as having been made in the Image of God. In Scripture, this designation is reserved *exclusively* for human beings.

Something We Do: The Functional View

Besides, the Bible says that *all* human beings have been created in God's Image. There is no hint of degrees, either before the Fall, or after.

There is another difficulty with the structural view. If being made in the Image of God means that we have a particular attribute or set of attributes, then what would we do if we found some non-human creature that had that same attribute or even the whole set of them?

Many behavioral scientists are quite confident that certain animals – dolphins, or chimpanzees, for instance – possess not only basic linguistic skills, but also the capacity for rational thought and abstract reasoning skills. These matters are highly debated, of course, but the very existence of the debate is worth noting.

Let's assume for a moment that some animals do possess one or more of these traits. What does this mean for the structural view of the Image of God?

Talking Apes?

When I am speaking on this topic to different audiences, I often begin the session by reading a fake newspaper article. I don't tell anyone it's a fake, of course. I just mention that I've found an interesting article and want to share it with everyone. The gist of the article is that primatologists (scientists who study apes) have finally proven that chimpanzees have the capacity for abstract thought and can express it in language. This is something that they've been studying for years, of course, but the evidence so far has been fairly ambivalent. In the fake article, however, I indicate that they've finally made a real breakthrough and that the chimp's capacity for rational thought and language usage is now a proven fact.

This is the most popular view of the Image of God in the Church today. However, there are significant weaknesses to this view.

Practically, this view struggles with what to make of human beings who do not seem to possess one or more of these attributes. Consider the genuine sociopath who seems to possess no innate sense of morality. Or, think about the unfortunate individual who was either born into, or has descended later in life into, a vegetative state in which rational thought, willpower or relational capacity seem to be nonexistent.

If we hold to the view that being made in the Image of God means that we possess certain attributes, there can be only one of two valid responses to such individuals. One option is to say that they only *appear* to be missing the attribute in question. In other words, the person in the vegetative state *is* rational, but we are unable to observe this, and the sociopath *does* have an innate moral capacity but simply refuses to acknowledge it. Now, that may be true in some cases, but that doesn't really solve the problem. The severely retarded individual may, in fact, be rational, but we have no way really of knowing this. The sociopath may be genuinely moral, struggling with a deeply repressed sense of guilt and anguish for their behavior, but there is no way to confirm or deny this fact.

In light of this difficulty, some people choose the second option: declaring that the Image of God is either *not* present in such handicapped individuals or is present, but to a lesser degree. Following this reasoning to its logical conclusion, then, we would have to believe smarter people are more in the Image of God than others.

Surely I do not need to waste any ink on the inherent danger of this idea. This lays the groundwork for all sorts of horrors; from indiscriminate euthanasia to wide-scale genocide.

God's sovereignty is obvious. The fact that we are intended to be His representatives is also clear, implied by our having been made in the Image of God. Unfortunately, this second truth is not as clear to us as it was to the original audience, because modern readers often hold to a distorted view of the *Imago Dei*. We must first rid ourselves of our misunderstandings so that we can see what Scripture really says quite plainly.

What does it mean to have been made in the Image of God? Most Christians hold to one of two views[14]. Some say that the Image is something we *have* while others say that the Image is something we *do*. The first is sometimes called the *structural* or the *substantive* view and the latter is often referred to as the *functional* view. Neither of these views is fully correct, but we must understand precisely where they fall apart so we can make room for the truth.

Something We Have: The Structural View

Most Christians today understand the Image of God in a structural sense. Those who hold to the structural view believe that the Image of God is something that human beings *possess*; in other words, the Image is something we have, usually identified as a particular human attribute or with a set of attributes.

The structural view says that being made in the Image of God means that we are rational, relational, moral, emotional ability or have free will. The structural view holds that it is one of these characteristics, or a set of such characteristics, which make us in the Image of God. Because we have these attributes, we are like God in certain respects.

14 For a review of all of the major interpretive options, see D.J.A. Clines, "The Image of God," *Tyndale Bulletin* (1968), 19:53-103.

Recognizing these difficulties with the structural understanding of the Image of God, some people have opted for a functional view. In this view, the Image of God is not something that humans *have*, but something that human beings *do*.

What is it we do that makes us the Image of God? Several options have been suggested[15], but the most common is the task of ruling and subduing the earth, since this is directly referred to in Genesis 1:26-28.

The functional view of the Image of God has at least two things in its favor.

First, if the Image of God is ever clearly explained in Scripture, we would expect it to be here in Genesis. The only apparent candidate for such an explanation is this notion of ruling, subduing, multiplying and filling.

Second, the functional view also avoids the potential difficulty of discovering that other creatures, either natural or supernatural, possess the traits discussed above. According to the functional view it is not the traits themselves which constitute the Image, but rather the task for which these capacities are to be used.

Unfortunately, the functional view ultimately suffers many of the same sorts of difficulties faced by the structural view. If we identify the Image of God as an action such as ruling, then what happens to the Image of God when we are not performing that action? What of individuals who, for various reasons are simply incapable of performing that action? Shall we say that

---

[15] Most recently, Stanley Grenz has popularized the idea that we are the Image of God because we form relationships with God and one another (*Theology For the Community of God* [Nashville: Broadman & Holman, 1994]). Grenz actually classifies this as a view distinct from the structural and the functional view, but I think it can fairly be understood as a sub-set of the functional view.

those who rule and subdue the earth with great vigor are more the Image of God than those who, for a variety of reasons, do so with less vigor or not at all?

Again, the Bible does not seem to allow this option. According to the Scriptures, every human being has been made in God's Image and there is no talk of degrees.

So where does that leave us? As is so often the case, I believe that the truth lies somewhere in between the extremes. Both the structural and the functional views are at least partially correct in their basic arguments, but they have not captured the whole picture.

The Representation View

To be made in the Image of God is partly something that we *have* and partly something that we *do*. These two pieces are inextricably intertwined. God has given us certain capacities because of what we have been made to *do* and we are able to do what we do because of those capacities that we *have been given*. In that sense, both the structural and the functional views are correct. However, rather than thinking of the Image of God as either something we have or something we do, I think we are much closer to the biblical concept when we speak of the Image of God as something that we *are*.

None of our various attributes constitute the Image of God. Neither does any particular task we have been assigned by God to do. These are all secondary considerations. I believe that the Image of God is something more basic and fundamental: *The Image of God is what we have been made to be.*

Individuals who lack certain attributes may be handicapped in their ability to perform their duties, so to speak, but this inability does not in any way change their innate status as the Image of God. At the same time, it is not all that troubling to find other creatures, be they chimpanzees or archangels, who possess some or even all of these basic capacities. It is not the capacities themselves which constitute the Image. The capacities are simply the attributes which are necessary for us to fulfill our purpose.

Now I realize that this notion runs contrary to many of our conceptions of what it means to be made in the Image of God and what I am proposing might not be crystal clear yet. Perhaps an illustration will be helpful.

The Intentions Of The Artist

Imagine that a sculptor sets himself to the task of making sculptures of Abraham Lincoln. For one he uses wax and creates the most life-like sculpture that he can produce, painting the wax with realistic flesh-tones. For another he uses marble. This sculpture is also life-like, but the artist doesn't paint it, so the sculpture remains basically white, though mottled by darker grains. For the third, the artist chooses to do a porcelain bust of Lincoln and artificially accentuates certain of Lincoln's facial features. Perhaps most of Lincoln's facial features are only vaguely represented, but the eyes are sculpted in full relief and rendered with a downward, humble look. The fourth work is an abstract piece: a big block of sandstone with the classic Lincoln top hat.

Now, which of these is a sculpture of Lincoln?

The answer, of course, is *all four*. The more life-like wax sculpture is not more of a sculpture of Lincoln than the marble statue sandstone cube. These are *all* sculptures of Lincoln.

Why? How can four works with such different appearances all be sculptures of Abraham Lincoln? Because it is the artist's *purpose* in creating them which determines what they are. It is the artist's intention which imparts to the objects their status as sculpture. The medium is irrelevant, as is the particular design.

Now, suppose all of our statues are on display in a museum and a fire breaks out. None of the sculptures is destroyed, but all are seriously damaged by the blaze. The marble statue breaks, losing an arm. The wax sculpture gets too hot and partially melts. The porcelain bust becomes charred and discolored. The sandstone blackens, cracks and distorts a bit.

Now which of these objects is a sculpture of Lincoln?

The answer, of course, is that they are *all still sculptures of Lincoln*. The fire may have distorted the degree to which they manifest their creator's original vision. The damage may have undermined their ability to fulfill their purpose. None of this, however, changes what they are. They were, and remain, sculptures of Lincoln. Damaged or intact, that is what they will always be.

Of course, it would be perfectly fair to ask how we would *recognize* these objects as sculptures of Lincoln. At this point, the various ways in which the statue represents their subject become important. Perhaps they depict the ubiquitous top hat. Maybe they all sport the scraggly beard. Perhaps they pay particular attention to the structure of his facial features. All of these are characteristics with are given to the sculptures so that they may serve their basic purpose. However, these characteristics are *not* what make these objects sculptures of Lincoln. Other sculptures may have a top hat or scraggly beard without having anything to do with Lincoln.

The sculptor might create his works hoping to evoke certain responses in his viewers. If his works *do* this for the viewers then it is functioning successfully, but such success or failure does not change what his sculptures are.

We *Are* The Image

In much the same way, we *are* the Image of God regardless of the characteristics we possess, the degree to which we possess them or the extent to which we fulfill the particular purpose for which God has made us. We are the Image of God because that is what we were made to be. Nothing can change the basic fact that we have been made to *be* the Image of God.

This may seem shocking, but that is only because we have learned some bad habits of thinking about this subject. This is illustrated, in part, by the fact that we often use inappropriate verbs in talking about the Image of God. We often say that human beings "reflect" the Image or that we "bear" the Image, but you will never find such notions in the Bible. Rather, in most cases, what you will find are verbs of *being*[16]:

> For a man ought not to have his head covered,
> since he *is* the image and glory of God; but the
> woman is the glory of man.
> (1 Corinthians 11:7)

This is also true in those verses where we find Jesus described as the perfect Image of God:

> He *is* the image of the invisible God, the
> firstborn of all creation.
> (Colossians 1:15)

The closest that the Bible comes to speaking of human beings bearing or reflecting the Image in some way is when it says that we were made "*in* the Image" (Gen. 1:26-27, 9:6).

---

[16] Now, these are New Testament verses, of course, and as such they were originally written in Greek, rather than the Hebrew we've been discussing. However, the Septuagint, a very important Greek translation of the O.T. which appeared sometime around 250 B.C., uses the word *eikon* to translate the Hebrew word *ts'lem* as found in Gen 1:26-28. This is the same Greek word translated as "image" in the two N.T. passages cited above.

However, the word "in" in these cases is derived from two different Hebrew prepositions, neither of which must be translated in this particular way. A perfectly acceptable, and I believe better, translation of this word is "as":

> Let us make man *as* our Image...
> For man has been made *as* the Image of God.

Again, I realize that this may sound presumptuous. Somehow, it seems less arrogant to think of having, bearing or reflecting the Image than to speak of *being* the Image. However, that is precisely how God's Word describes us.

Part of the problem is that the English word "image" implies something that is not necessarily intended by the original Hebrew and Greek words. The English word "image" implies a *reproduction*...something that looks just like the original.

That is not necessarily the case with the Hebrew and Greek terms. The original words were less concerned with ideas of reproduction and more concerned with ideas of *representation*.

The Importance Of The Body

Let me ask you this: what is the one thing that humans possess which no other creatures do? Think about it for a moment.

Chances are good that you have thought of the soul or spirit. In fact, this is often one of the candidates put forth by structuralist view as being the critical attribute which makes us the Image of God. It is apparently true that human beings possess a soul/spirit[17] and other animals do not, but of course angels have spirits as well. In fact, they *are* spirits! So, it cannot be that our role as the Image of God depends on our having souls.

Actually, there is no one thing which the human being possesses but which no other creature has. However, there is one particular combination of things which makes us unique from all other creatures: *we are embodied spirits*. We have an immaterial spirit that is contained within a physical body. Animals apparently do not have souls and angels do not have bodies[18]. Only human beings occupy this particular niche in Creation.

Our bodies are an integral part of our role as the Image of God. *To be made in the Image of God is intimately connected to our physical nature.*

Now, I am aware that many people will have an immediate negative reaction to this statement. However, this is a thoroughly biblical concept. In fact, I believe this is really the only way to understand the notion of the Image of God. To do otherwise is to do severe injustice to the basic interpretive principles of reading in context, and understanding words according to their common meaning within the rest of Scripture.

---

[17] I consider the words "soul" and "spirit" to be technically synonymous. It is true that 1Th. 5:23 and Heb. 4:12 seem to speak of body, soul and spirit as three distinct elements, but they appear to do so in a non-technical sense; that is, these appear to be statements couched in the common vernacular. In every other case where "spirit" and "soul" occur together, speaking of the human constitution, they are clearly synonymous terms used for stylistic variation. (1Sa. 1:15, Job 7:11, Isa. 26:9)

[18] True, angels may manifest themselves on occasion in physical form, but they do not possess bodies in their natural state. In the same way, human spirits live on after death, awaiting the resurrection, but again this is not their natural state.

The Hebrew words for "image" and "likeness" in Genesis 1:26-28 are used frequently throughout the Bible. They are not rare, though their use in relationship to human beings is somewhat limited. These words always have one basic meaning: a *physical* representation of someone/something, often of something or someone with power or authority.

In fact, the Hebrew words translated as "image" and "likeness" (*ts'lem* and *de'mot*, if you're interested) are typically used in the Bible to designate *idols*. Now, what could that possibly have to do with us? Idols are statues that people worship in stead of worshipping the true God, right?

Well, not exactly. We often suffer from a serious case of what I call temporal snobbery; that is, we often think, because we live later in history, that we are the intellectual superiors of the "primitives" that lived in ancient times. The notion of idol worship seems to cement our opinion of them. What could be more primitive than worshipping statues and figurines? How could anyone think that a statue made by human hands was worthy of worship?

The answer to that question is: *they didn't*; didn't think that the statues themselves were worthy of worship, that is. Rather, what they thought was that the statues were physical representations of gods or spirit beings who demanded worship.

From the human vantage point, idols were a means of representing the gods, of providing a focal point for the worship of them. From the vantage point of the gods and goddesses, idols were a means of mediating[19] their presence in the physical world. In other words, the idols served as an intermediary between the spirits and the physical world. As physical objects imbued with spiritual significance (and sometimes power) the

---

[19] That is, a means by which the gods and goddesses made their presence known and felt in the physical world.

idols were thought to be a juxtaposition between the physical and spiritual worlds.

Now whenever I teach this, one of the immediate questions that arises is this: are you telling me that people didn't *worship* idols?

The answer to that question is both yes and no. Keep in mind that the most important Biblical words for worship, both in Greek and Hebrew, refer to the literal act of bowing in submission. So, yes, they built shrines around the idols and bowed down before them. In this respect, they certainly did worship the idols[20]. However, these acts of worship were not directed to the statues themselves, but to the spirits who were thought to stand *behind* them, so to speak. So, no, they did not worship the idols so much as the gods and goddesses that the various idols represented.

They didn't think the statues were gods themselves.

It would also be inaccurate to suggest that the shape of the idols was thought to reflect the literal appearance of the gods they represented. Rather, an idol was fashioned in such a way as to symbolically represent some aspect or aspects of a deity's character. The Hindu god Vishnu, for instance, is usually depicted with at least four arms, not because the Hindis believe she has four literal arms, but because the arms represent Vishnu's supposed influence over multiple realms[21].

---

[20] And the physical idols themselves were often greatly revered, much like the ancient Hebrews sometimes revered the Ark of the Covenant, even going so far as to think that God could be manipulated into acting so as to save His holy object from capture by the Philistines (cf. 1 Samuel 4).

[21] The precise identification of these four realms varies considerably. Sometimes they are thought to be the four realms of space. Sometimes they are thought to be the four stages of human life (Ashrams) or the four aims of life (Purusharthas). Other interpreters speak of two of the arms symbolizing her control over the physical world and the other two symbolizing her

The shape of the idol was of secondary importance. In fact, the very idol itself was of only limited importance. It was the unseen spirits themselves that were thought to be worthy of worship. But, ancient people believed that these gods used these idols to mediate their presence to the world. They were a focus of worship, but the figures themselves were not intrinsically worthy of worship. They were valuable because they were a means by which the gods supposedly mediated or manifested their presence in the world.

The Hebrew and Greek words for "idol" are the same terms used to describe human beings as made in God's Image.

Why?

Because God made for the same purpose: *to represent God in creation and mediate His presence here.* We are the physical representatives of God in creation. We were made to be this and we remain this. We will always be this...in fact, that's why the separation of soul and body at death must be a temporary thing. We exist as disembodied spirits only for a time until our souls are reunited with our glorified and resurrected bodies:

> In this way also is the resurrection of the dead; sown in weakness, raised in imperishability; sown in dishonor, raised in glory; sown in weakness, raised in power, sown an unspiritual body, raised a spiritual body. If there is an unspiritual body, there is also a spiritual one.
>
> (1 Corinthians 15:42-44)

> Blessed and holy is the one who has a place in the first resurrection. Over them the second death will have no authority, but they will be

---

control over the spiritual world. In some cases, Vishnu is depicted with even more arms in order to symbolize her even wider sphere of influence.

priests of God and of Christ and will reign with
him for a thousand years.

(Revelation 20:6)

One of the common misconceptions that I encounter about
heaven is that we will be some sort of disembodied spirits,
floating around in the presence of God. This is not what the
Bible teaches. Scripture is very clear that at Jesus' return we
will be given new physical bodies. Why? Because without
them, we cannot do what we were made to do.

Kingdom Assignments

And what, exactly, is it that we were made to do? We see
hints of it in Revelation 20:6 quoted above. Do you see the two
things there that we're told we will do with Christ at his return?
We will be "priests of God and of Christ" and we will "reign
with him for a thousand years."

These two functions may be described as *mediation* and
representation.

As priests, we will be mediators. Mediation means that we
will serve as a means by which God manifests His presence in
the world. During the Millennium, God will demonstrate His
presence, His character and His will to the rest of the world, in
part, through believers. That we will be priests also implies that
we will serve as go-betweens for the unbelievers and for God.
This was the basic role of a priest in the Old Testament. At that
time, priests made the sacrifices and interceded before God for
the people. They were the go-betweens. During the
Millennium, all believers will serve in this role, although, of
course, there will be no need of sacrifices.

However, we will not be simple priests. We will be *royal*
priests, for we will also reign with Him. Now this presents an

interesting question, for I take it to be self-evident that God does not, indeed cannot, actually share His throne with anyone. So in what sense can we reign with Him?

I take this to mean that we serve as representatives of God, royal ambassadors[22] who carry out the will of their King, and who also have been delegated some of His authority and power for that purpose. The term "ambassador" is perhaps not quite strong enough since this passage and others like it seem to imply something more similar to regency. An ambassador simply represents the interest of another. A regent, on the other hand, is one who actually rules an area in the name of a greater authority.

In Genesis 1, God's absolute sovereignty is expressed in two ways.

First, God speaks and His word is carried out:

> Then God said, "Let there be light"; and there
> was light.
>
> (Genesis 1:1)

This pattern is repeated ten times in the first chapter of Genesis and is a clear portrayal of God's role as the ultimate sovereign. When most people want something to happen, what do they have to do? They have to work hard to get it done. Who gets things done just by commanding that they be done? Only those with great power and authority. That all of creation sprang into existence at God's spoken command is an indication of His absolute sovereignty.

Second, God's sovereignty is expressed in His right to name things, or in some cases, to re-name things, as we see Him doing throughout Scripture:

---

[22] For a thorough treatment of Christians as ambassadors of God and Christ, see Anthony Bash, *Ambassadors for Christ* (Tubingen: J.C.B. Mohr, 1997).

"No longer shall your name be called Abram,
but your name shall be Abraham; for I will
make you the father of a multitude of nations."
(Genesis 17:5)

And Jesus said to him, "Blessed are you, Simon
Barjona, because flesh and blood did not reveal
this to you, but My Father who is in heaven. I
also say to you that you are Peter, and upon this
rock I will build My church; and the gates of
Hades will not overpower it."
(Matthew 16:17-18)

In the Ancient Near East, names were extremely important.
Names were believed to have power. That is one of the reasons
that the Hebrew people didn't speak God's name aloud. To do
could easily have been understood as an attempt to exercise
control over God. At the very least, it would have been seen as
extremely disrespectful, like a teenager meeting the president of
the United States and calling him "Georgie."

Even modern American culture retains a hint of this respect
for names. Children are generally expected to address adults as
"Mr. Smith" or "Mrs. Swanson" rather than use their first
names. Unless given permission to do otherwise, college
students address the faculty by their titles, like Professor or
Doctor. So, even in our extremely casual culture, we have some
remnant of this belief that the way we use peoples' names has
something to do with their rank in society relative to our own.
In the same way, but to a much higher degree, in the Hebrew
culture, names were closely associated with rank and power.

Consequently, the greatest sign of rank was the ability to
determine names. Children don't give names to parents.

Parents, who have authority over children, determine what their names will be. The ability to name something is indicative of our authority over it. And so it is that in Genesis 1, God's right to name everything in creation is an intentional portrayal of His sovereignty over everything.

Now, here's where things get interesting. Having made Adam to be His representative in creation, God gave Adam a specific task. Do you remember what it was?

Adam's first act as the Imago Dei was to *name* the animals:

> Out of the ground the LORD God formed every beast of the field and every bird of the sky, and brought them to the man to see what he would call them; and whatever the man called a living creature, that was its name.
>
> (Genesis 2:19)

God's willingness to allow Adam the right to name His creation is an expression of the fact that God has delegated His royal authority to him. Not all of it, of course, for we are not co-equal with God by any stretch of the imagination. What Adam was, however, was a regent: one appointed to rule via the delegated power and authority of the higher sovereign.

Of course, this should come as no surprise, since this is precisely what God Himself expressed as His purpose for human beings:

> "Let Us make man in Our image, according to Our likeness; and *let them rule* over the fish of the sea and over the birds of the sky and over the cattle and over all the earth, and over every creeping thing that creeps on the earth."
>
> (Genesis 1:26)

We rule not by our own authority, of course, but on the basis of *delegated* authority.

This is the purpose of human existence. This is what we were made to be: God's representatives in creation, delegated whatever power, ability, authority and characteristics are necessary to function in this capacity.

This does not necessarily mean that we are the only beings God has made to represent Him. In fact, angels are frequently depicted in Scripture as functioning in this capacity. So we are not necessarily God's only representatives. However, we are the only *physical* representatives.

Think about it for a moment. If the United States needed to send an ambassador to China, what qualifications would we look for? Loyalty and trustworthiness would certainly be important. Having a sound grasp of U.S. policy and interests would be critical as well. Other qualities such as intelligence, wisdom and charisma would probably be important considerations also. But say we had two candidates who were virtually equal in all these respects. How would we choose between them? It might be difficult, but say one of them spoke fluent Chinese and the other did not. Furthermore, what if that one was of Chinese ancestry? Leaving aside any possible loyalty issues, is the choice so difficult anymore?

Of course not. The best ambassadors are the ones who are most able to relate to their constituents. And we are always able to relate best to those who are like us in important ways. So, when God created the physical universe, what better representatives could He fashion than those who were like Him in some respects but who also like the creation? Simply put, a physical world needs physical ambassadors. Of course, God didn't "select" us to be His ambassadors, as though He had to choose between several candidates. He made us uniquely for this purpose.

To be made in God's Image, then, is inherently connected to being physical. That is why the very words God chose to use in describing us are terms typically found describing other kinds of physical representations. I believe this is also part of why we are forbidden to make physical images of God...because *we* are the physical representations of God[23]. Not, of course, in the sense that we actually *look* like God, but in the sense that we are embodied spirits intended to represent Him, to mediate His presence, in the creation.

As such, we have been delegated capacities and assigned duties by which to represent Him. We cannot fulfill our purpose without rational thought, emotional ability, relational capacity, etc... nor can we fulfill our purpose without ruling and subduing the creation over which we were made stewards. The Fall, with all its accompanying dysfunctions, has kept us from fulfilling our purpose, in part because it has radically impacted both our capacities and the uses to which we put them. To return to our sculpture analogy, however, these are simply the means by which our status as the Image of God is *recognizable*, The extent to which we possess such capacities and things we use them for do not affect our innate status as God's Image.

The Image & The Fall

Though the word "Kingdom" does not occur in the first chapter of Genesis, the concept is actually a central feature. For in the opening scene of the great drama of God's eternal plan for humanity, we learn that we were made to function in His Image, as His physical representatives in creation. In order to

---

[23] Another important reason for the prohibition seems to be the fact that casting "graven images" of God would lead naturally to conceiving of God in similar terms to other, pagan deities. One of the constant struggles the Israelites faced was the temptation to think of God as one among many, rather than as the only, absolutely unique God.

do this, we were made both like God and like the world in which we are to be His ambassadors.

The great tragedy, of course, is that we have "gone native." Abandoning our intended role as God's representatives in the world, we have chosen to live for the creation, rather than for the Creator. Is it any wonder, then, that God sees sin in such a harsh light? Sin is not just rebellion, it is high treason against the very King in whose Image we were made!

How exactly did the Fall affect the Image of God? We have already seen that our status as the Image of God rests entirely on God's intention for us. As such, the Image was not lost at the Fall. The fact that God continues to refer to post-Fall human beings as His Image clearly illustrates this fact:

> "Whoever sheds man's blood, by man his blood
> shall be shed, For in the image of God He made
> man."
>
> (Genesis 9:6)

> For a man ought not to have his head covered,
> since he is the image and glory of God;
>
> (1 Corinthians 11:7)

The Fall did not cause us to cease to be the Image of God. However, it has certainly affected the way we function as God's ambassadors. Simply put, we do not represent God *well*. Our lives no longer clearly reflect our King's character and will.

In part, this is due to the fact that sin has broken our relationship with God. When Adam and Eve sinned, they were banished from the Garden and from the intimate fellowship they had enjoyed with their Creator. With broken relationships come broken lines of communication. We are like ambassadors who can no longer call home. We don't know how to function as representatives because we don't know what our King is like and we can't find out.

In Christ, of course, this all changes. Jesus said:

> "You are My friends if you do what I command you. No longer do I call you slaves, for the slave does not know what his master is doing; but I have called you friends, for all things that I have heard from My Father I have made known to you."
>
> (John 15:14-15)

Obviously, if we are Jesus' friends only so long as we obey his commands, then Jesus does not have in mind the same kind of friendship that we might immediately think of. In what sense are we his friends? In the sense that we are no longer *slaves*. Slaves are expected to do what their master commands. The master has absolutely no obligation to explain his commands or let the slaves know how their work fits into the big picture. But here, Jesus calls us friends because he is making the Father's plans known to us. We have been brought into God's circle of confidence.

As we come to understand the King and His plans for the Kingdom, we grow more and more able to function effectively as His Image. This is, at least partially, what is meant when Paul speaks of Christians being *transformed* into the Image of Christ:

> But we all, with unveiled face, beholding as in a mirror the glory of the Lord, are being transformed into the same image...
>
> (2 Corinthians 3:18)

Jesus is said to be the "image of the invisible God" (Col. 1:15) because he is the perfect illustration of what God is like. He is God incarnate. At the same time, though, he is fully human and, as such, he is the perfect role model of what were made to be. As we grow in Christlikeness, we become more effective in fulfilling our God-ordained purpose. Call it *transformational restoration*. Like an old portrait restored to its former glory by the careful attention of an expert, in Christ, we are transformed from what we have become to what we once were. And who better to restore a work of art than the original Artist.

The Fall tarnished every aspect of our ability to represent God. Our intellect, our relationships, our emotions, and everything else have been tainted by sin. Our bodies as well, that aspect of our makeup that allows us to represent God in creation, have been radically affected by the Fall. The ultimate consequence of our sin is death (Gen. 2:17). Death is both physical and spiritual. Spiritually, we are separated from God who is the source of all life. Physically, our bodies break down and our souls are left homeless…until the resurrection.

The Fall has also affected the world over which we were given regency. From this understanding about human nature we begin to see why there is such evil rampant in the world today. We are not mere citizens in rebellion, we are apostate ambassadors, renegade regents. Think of it this way: an American tourist wandering around Beijing can do some damage. Insensitivity and arrogance on the part of such an individual can give some Chinese a negative impression of the United States. That's not good, of course, but the damage is limited. But what if that same insensitivity and arrogance came from the U.S. ambassador to China? Now the damage is far worse. In the same way, the abilities and even the authority delegated to us by the King have put us in a position to do tremendous harm, to one another and to our world. Why God has not chosen to strip us of our rank and divest us of the privileges of that position is an enduring mystery to me, but He has not. In many ways we are like small children with power tools; we have great potential, but the uses to which we put it usually precipitate disaster.

Conclusion

We were made to represent the King and His Kingdom. As we have seen in this chapter, such a notion is to be found in the very first words of Holy Scripture. And, it remains a central theme right up to the last words of John's Revelation. If anything, this theme is intensified in the New Testament.

FIVE

In The King's Name

The pulpit is both the thrill and the threat in any pastor's work. Oh the joy of sharing the Word of God and oh the fear that you might inadvertently say in the name of God what God never intended to say!

It was my turn in the pulpit, but I wasn't thrilled about it.

I love preaching, and though the task of biblical interpretation and sermon preparation is time-consuming and mentally taxing, I love the work. The passage for this week, however, was driving me insane. I'm a "big idea" preacher, which means that I think a unit of biblical text generally has one main idea. My job as preacher is to get that idea across to the congregation clearly: to make sure they understand it and know how to apply it. Determining the big idea that God intends to communicate through a particular passage takes work, but it's not usually all that hard. Every now and then, though...

We were preaching through Luke's Gospel and the passage which fell to me on this particular Sunday was Luke 9:46-62. You may be familiar with this section of Scripture, but there's a pretty good chance you've never thought of it as cohesive unit. I certainly didn't when I first looked at it. In fact, when I first began to study these verses, my impression was that Luke had cobbled together several unrelated incidents from Jesus' life and stuck them together at random.

I knew that wasn't the case, of course. Nothing about God's word is random or unimportant, but this particular passage really had me confused.

As I began to look at the text more carefully, however, it became clear that the passage was intended to be read as a single unit. There were several grammatical indicators that linked the various pieces together. But it was still a strange conglomeration.

The passage begins with a typical disagreement among the disciples. Actually, it wasn't the disciples generally, mind you, but the "inner core" that we know as the apostles. It would be nice to say they were having a vigorous debate about deep theological issues, but they weren't. They were having an argument about which of them was the greatest.

Now, we often view this argument as proof of what a bunch of *yahoos* the apostles were. How could they possibly have been hanging out with Jesus Christ himself, day in and day out, and still be so self-centered?

Actually, it's not quite that bad. The apostles saw Jesus, among other things, in terms of a rabbi and themselves as his disciples. Jesus wasn't exactly a rabbi, of course, at least not in a technical sense. He had no official position of authority within the framework of Jewish society. Still, his teaching, preaching and gathering disciples looked more rabbinic than anything else, so it was natural for his closest associates to think of him in similar terms. Given that framework, it would have been quite natural to ask which of them would take up the baton, so to speak, when the Master stepped down. The greatest Jewish teachers typically stood at the head of a particular tradition or school of thought, and they always had one special disciple who carried on their teaching after they retired. This did not necessarily mean that the teacher's other disciples were inferior, only that this one disciple was chosen to receive the very special honor of carrying on the teacher's work after he was gone.

Certainly there was still some pride hanging out at the edges of the conversation when Jesus' disciples began to wonder which of them was to be the "greatest," but the discussion itself isn't so immature as it may seem to a modern reader.

It is worth noting, as well, that just prior to the disciples' argument, Jesus had just announced that "...the Son of Man is going to be delivered into the hands of men" (Lk. 9:44). Luke explicitly tells us that the disciples didn't understand what he meant, but the announcement apparently got them thinking that Jesus wouldn't always be around. Seen in that light, their ensuing discussion makes a certain amount of sense.

In Jesus' Name

What is curious, however, is Jesus' response:

> Jesus, knowing what they were thinking in their heart, took a child and stood him by His side, and said to them, "Whoever receives this child in My name receives Me, and whoever receives Me receives Him who sent Me; for the one who is least among all of you, this is the one who is great."
>
> (Luke 9:47-48)

Now, we've probably all heard this part of the passage preached a number of times and because of that, we may have started to lose our ability to see what an odd thing it is. If Jesus had told his disciples to grow up, get over it and stop looking for ways to exalt themselves, we wouldn't be surprised, would we? We wouldn't be astonished if he had taken this child and said only the part about "the one who is least among all of you, this is the one who is great." Those kind of responses would have made sense.

But what's this business of receiving the child "in My name"? And how is it that receiving a child like that is equivalent to receiving Jesus? And what is this about receiving Jesus being equivalent to receiving the one who sent him? Of course, on one level this is a statement that Jesus is intimately connected to God the Father, but why is Jesus talking about this connection right now? What does this have to do with which of the disciples will represent Jesus after he's gone? It seems like a strange response to the disciple's conversation, doesn't it?

If *that* seems strange, look at John's response to Jesus' statement:

> "Master, we saw someone casting out demons in
> Your name; and we tried to prevent him because
> he does not follow along with us."
>
> (Luke 9:48)

Huh?

What's going on here? Wasn't John listening to Jesus? Here Jesus has just taught this profound thing about the least being the greatest and he has provided everyone with such a poignant illustration with this dear child right by his side. And John responds by saying, basically, "Um….Jesus, there was this guy, see? He was casting out demons in your name, okay? But the thing is, he isn't one of us, so we tried to stop him."

What in the world does this have to do with what Jesus had just said?

When I first read this, I didn't have a clue. I'm sure I had read it many times before, but the apparent incongruity had never struck me. Now that I was trying to figure out what God was saying here so that I could preach it, however, the incongruity struck me and struck me hard.

My first reaction, as I've already said, was to think that these were unrelated incidents that just happened to be sitting next to each other in the text as Luke presents it to us. On closer inspection, however, it becomes clear that there is something that connects Jesus' teaching to John's question. Do you see it?

It's the phrases "in my name" and "in your name." John had heard Jesus quite clearly, but what the Master said had reminded him of something. John was seeking some clarification.

The key to the connection between these events is this "in My name" business. So, what do "in my name" and "in your name" mean? That's the question I began to ask once I realized that it was what connected these bits of the text. As long as I had a solid grasp on this, I reasoned, the passage would become clear and I'd be able to get down to the work of figuring out how to preach it.

Trouble was, I realized, I didn't really know.

What's In A Name?

Does that surprise you? It sure surprised me! After all, we Christians use basically the same phrase all the time. "In My name" and "in Your name" are both variants of a typical phrase found throughout the New Testament: *in the name of Jesus.* We employ the same phrase at the end of almost every prayer, don't we? Since it's such a common phrase, I should have known precisely what it meant.

But I realized that I didn't.

Oh, I thought I did, but as I considered the way I typically used the phrase, it became evident that they didn't make sense in this particular context. After contemplating the question for a while, I decided to see if other people thought about "in the name of Jesus" along the same lines that I did. So, I got on the phone and started calling people from the church directory pretty much at random.

Without exception, everyone's answers fell perfectly in line with what I'd always thought as well. The problem was that our typical understandings of the phrase didn't fit the context of this passage at all.

Just about every answer fell into one of two categories. The first category, and most common answer, was that "in the name of Jesus" meant that we were able to pray *because* of what Jesus did for us. In other words, because Jesus died on the cross and opened the way to God, we were able to pray and know that we were heard. Jesus was the back-stage pass, in a manner of speaking, to God's presence.

Now, it's true that Jesus provides our access to God and makes possible our acceptance by Him. Our faith is firmly rooted in His work and it is only by His work that our relationships with the Father are possible. But this cannot be what "in the name of Jesus" means in the context of Luke's gospel, for several reasons.

To begin with, Jesus hadn't completed that work yet when he first spoke these words. He hadn't gone to the cross. He hadn't torn the Temple veil. So, to understand the phrase this way requires that we read it like this: "If you receive this child…on the basis of the work that I haven't done yet and you don't really have any clue that I'm going to do, but I *will* do it and then it will clear the way to God making it possible for you to come to Him…then you will be receiving me!" Obviously, that's ridiculous.

Further, while Jesus' work did provide access to God, it doesn't explain how we would end up receiving Jesus *himself* by receiving a child on the basis of work which the Lord did on our behalf. Finally, understanding the phrase this way makes utter nonsense out of John's question about the itinerant exorcist.

"Lord," John was essentially saying, "we saw this guy casting out demons *on the basis of your work and power*, but we tried to stop him." Does that make any sense? Obviously, John's question demonstrates that he understood the phrase in question to mean something different.

The second category of answer that I got in response to my informal survey was this: to do anything "in the name of Jesus" was to do it *according to the will of Jesus* (i.e. to do things that are in line with His desires and plans).

Now, this makes a certain amount of sense, at least in regard to the child: if we receive a child because Jesus wants us to, then we will have, in some sense, received Jesus. A bit odd perhaps, but not completely without sense. But again, John's question about the itinerant exorcist shows this type of answer to be wrong as well. What was he saying? "Jesus, we saw this guy casting out demons *according to your will*, but don't worry…we tried to stop him!" Does that make any sense? Of course not!

So where does that leave us?

Well, it left me a bit confused. Here was a phrase that is spread through our Christian-talk like Barbie accessories in a four-year old girl's room and I suddenly realized that I didn't really know what it meant.

It was John's response that kept nagging at me. What did John know about the phrase "in the name of" that I didn't? What was it about the phrase that triggered this particular question?

It seemed clear that both John and Jesus were operating out of a common understanding of the phrase; that they both knew what it meant because it was a phrase with which they were both quite familiar. So, I turned to the historical records of the first century and started looking for uses of this phrase in the literature from that period. And you know what? I found a lot of them.

There were two general contexts in which the phrase occurred: the political and the commercial. In both contexts, the phrase was used in basically the same way. As I looked at these uses, the meaning of the phrase became abundantly clear. To be honest, I felt like an idiot for not having seen it before.

These are words of *representation*.

Commercially, the phrase "in the name of" occurred when people were doing business on behalf of someone else. For instance, say a man had traveled to the city of Ephesus to conduct business for his employer, who remained behind in Rome. In the business negotiations the employee was said to act "in the name of" his employer. In other words, the employee was to act as though he was the employer.

We have a similar legal arrangement in the U.S. today. It's called *Power of Attorney*. When Power of Attorney has been bestowed on, or delegated to, someone, that person is authorized to sign documents and conduct business *as though they were the person in question*. When Coletta and I bought our first house in Colorado, we discovered that the cost of real estate (if you can call our postage-stamp sized yard real *estate*) was staggering. Since Coletta hadn't yet signed a teaching contract and I was taking a job part-time while I attended seminary, our income on paper didn't qualify us for a large enough loan. So, my parents co-signed on the mortgage for us. They lived in Ohio, though, and it didn't make sense for them to come out to Colorado just to sign the loan papers at closing. So, they filled out some forms granting me Power of Attorney. At the closing, I signed their names. The signatures were accepted as legally binding because, due to the Power of Attorney, I was acting "in the name of" my parents; that is, as though I were them. This was precisely the way the phrase "in the name of" was used even in ancient commercial contexts.

In the ancient literature, though, commercial uses of this phrase are relatively uncommon when compared to the phrase's *political* uses. The meaning, however, was still the same. Ambassadors went out "in the name of" kings and rulers. They negotiated treaties and announced taxes, but not on the basis of their own power and authority. Rather, these ambassadors carried out their duties with power and authority that accorded to them by the rulers they represented. When they arrived in foreign courts, they were honored and respected because they came "in the name of" their lieges; that is, they were treated almost as though they were kings themselves.

We have the same thing today. When we send an ambassador to, say, China, that man or woman represents the United States of America in that foreign land. They are afforded great power and authority to conduct business "in the name of" the United States. They become, in essence, a singular, visible representative of the U.S. on Chinese soil.

To do something "in the name of" someone means to do it as a representative of that individual.

Suddenly the passage in Luke 9:42-66 became clear. Both Jesus and John were acting out of a common understanding of what the phrase "in the name of" meant.

"Listen," said Jesus. "If you receive this child as a representative of me, then you will have received me."

"And," he continued, "if you receive me, then you will have received the one who sent me." Why? Because Jesus Christ is the visible representative of the invisible God (Col. 1:15)…his entire ministry was conducted *in the name of* the Father, who sent Him.

The Cause Of The Confusion

John's odd response to Jesus suddenly made a lot more sense as well. "That reminds me of something I'd been meaning to ask you about, Jesus," he basically said. "See, there was this guy casting out demons as though he represented you, but we tried to stop him because he's not one of us." What John meant, of course, was that this man was not part of the inner circle. He hadn't been delegated any authority as far as John was aware.

"Don't stop him", Jesus said. "If he's not against you, he's for you." *"Come on, guys!"* Jesus seems to be saying. *"Did he* try *to cast out demons 'in my name' or did he actually* do *it? Actually did it, huh? Where do you figure he got the power to do that?"*

In Acts 19:13, we're told of a group of Jewish exorcists who tried to cast out a demon *in Jesus' name* only to be physically beaten by it and sent running away naked. Actually, what they said was, "In the name of Jesus, whom Paul preaches, I command you to come out." As the demon remarked prior to the thrashing, "Jesus I know, and I know about Paul, but who are you?" The meaning is clear. These men had no actual authority from the one in whose name they tried to operate. They had no "Power of Attorney" so to speak!

Here in Luke 9, however, the man the disciples were talking about apparently *succeeded.* God honored his attempted exorcism with divine power and actually cast the demons out.

This, Scripture tells us, is one of powers that Jesus delegates to his true disciples. "If you've seen him be successful," Jesus told them, "and if he's not against you, then doesn't it stand to reason that he's *with* you...that he's one of you?"

But you see, here lies the crux of the issue for the disciples. They were trying to figure out which of the inner circle would carry on the message of Jesus and here they were told that even a tag-along, one of the guys hanging out on the fringe of Jesus' coat-tails, was allowed and empowered to function as Jesus' representative.

This is an idea that is expanded on in the next section:

> When the days were approaching for His ascension, He was determined to go to Jerusalem; and He sent messengers on ahead of Him, and *they* went and entered a village of the Samaritans to make arrangements for Him. But they did not receive *Him*, because He was traveling toward Jerusalem. [emphasis mine]
>
> (Luke 9:51-53)

Not to get too technical here, but do you notice the odd interplay of pronouns here? He sent messengers ahead of *him...they* went into the village...but the village did not receive *him*. The village rejected Jesus even though Jesus himself never actually arrived in the village...only the messengers did. How can they have rejected Jesus personally if they only saw the messengers? Because, the messengers functioned "in the name of" Jesus.

It was as though the messengers were Jesus himself. By rejecting the messengers, they rejected the one who sent them. Between God's arrangement of the historical events and His inspiration of Luke's arrangement of the text, we are presented here with a clever reversal of the lesson Jesus just taught his disciples: *if you receive a representative of me you will have received me and if you receive me you will have received the One who sent me.*

By rejecting the representatives of Jesus, the Samaritan village rejected Jesus himself. The disciples, fully realizing the dishonor implied by this rejection suggested doing what any good Old Testament prophet would have done after receiving

such shoddy treatment: call down fire upon the village as
punishment. Jesus demurred, telling them that they didn't quite
understand yet what he was all about:

> "You do not know what kind of spirit you are
> of; for the Son of Man did not come to destroy
> men's lives, but to save them."
>
> (Lk. 9:55-56)

See how this seemingly fragmented passage hangs together
beautifully once we understand the historical and cultural
meaning of the phrase "in the name of"? The disciples were
arguing about who would be the greatest...about who would
represent Jesus' movement when he was out of the picture.
Jesus responded by teaching them that even those perceived by
the world as insignificant could serve as his representatives and
that they should accept them accordingly. John wanted to know
if that included someone on the fringe of the movement and
Jesus indicates that it does. Finally, the significance of
representing Jesus is further underscored by the report that a
Samaritan village's rejection of Jesus' messengers was
equivalent to rejecting the Lord himself.

All who follow Jesus become representatives of him. This
notion of representing Jesus is a common theme in Luke's
Gospel. For instance, in Luke 10 we find the story of Jesus
preaching to the seventy-two disciples that he was sending out
to proclaim the Kingdom of God. Part of the instruction was
this:

> "The one who listens to you listens to me; he
> who rejects you rejects me; but he who
> rejects me rejects him who sent me."
>
> (Luke 10:16)

Here we find a reiteration of the lesson we just looked at from Luke 9. All who follow Jesus, not just the apostles, have the privilege of serving as representatives of the Lord.

This is also a central theme in the Luke's book of Acts.

Stephen: Glorified Waiter?

In the book of Acts, we find such things as the apostles rejoicing at their flogging by the Sanhedrin because they had been "counted worthy of suffering disgrace for the Name" (Acts 5:41). They weren't thrilled about the persecution, of course. I doubt very much that they stumbled out saying to one another, "*I* got eleven lashes…how many did *you* get?!"

They rejoiced not in the persecution itself, but in the fact that the persecution was proof that their allegiance to, and representation of, Jesus, was beyond doubt.

The problem, though, is that the apostles still seemed to think of representing Jesus as exclusively *their* privilege.   In Acts 6, when a complaint arose in the early church because certain widows were being overlooked in the "daily distribution of food" the apostles made an interesting statement: "It would not be right for us to neglect the ministry of the word of God in order to wait on tables." (Acts 6:2) Now, this is an interesting statement on several levels.

It is interesting, in part, because the whole affair has some eerie similarities to the time that the disciples went to Jesus and asked him to send the crowds away so everyone could get some food (Luke 9:12-17). Do you remember Jesus' response to them? Jesus replied to them: "You give them something to eat."   There are some interesting grammatical and thematic elements that seem to indicate that Luke wanted his readers to see a connection between the incident in Luke 9 and the one in Acts 6. But in Acts 6, the apostles still seem to be struggling with Jesus' instruction. Rather than giving those in need the food, they opt to have someone else "wait on tables."

Ironically, we never actually see the seven men who were selected to "wait on tables" do so. I'm sure they did, but Luke goes out of his way to tell us other things about these men. One of them, Philip, was involved in the first Gentile conversion to the faith and another, Stephen, became the first martyr for the faith.

The story of Stephen is very important, particularly in the context of Luke's ongoing theme of believers as representatives of Jesus. God both orchestrated events, and inspired Luke to record them in a particular way so that the association between Stephen and Jesus was obvious. If you look at the events recorded between Acts 6:8 and 7:59, several clear parallels emerge:

1. Both Stephen and Jesus performed wonders and miraculous signs

2. Both Stephen and Jesus were persecuted by their own people (Jesus by the Jews and his townsfolk in Nazareth, Stephen by members of the Synagogue of the Freedmen, to which he belonged)

3. Both Stephen and Jesus were accused of a particular sin: blasphemy

4. In both cases, these men were accused in relationship to the claim that Jesus would destroy the "temple" and raise it again

5. Both were brought before the Sanhedrin

6. False witnesses were produced to accuse both men

7. Both men were killed for their claims

8. Some of Jesus' last words were "Father, forgive them, for they do not know what they are doing" and "Father, into your hands I commit my spirit." Stephen's last words were "Lord Jesus, receive my spirit" and "Lord, do not hold this sin against them."

The point of all this similarity is quite simple. Stephen, though he was selected to wait on tables, also had the same privilege as the apostles of representing Jesus. In fact, if the apostles considered it an honor to be flogged for the name of Jesus, then Stephen's honor was greater.

N.T. Wright, a very important contemporary New Testament scholar, once said that the Acts of the Apostles should be renamed "The Reluctant Acts of the Apostles." I think he's right. In many ways, the book of Acts details their painful learning of lessons that should have been clear from the teaching that they had received directly from Jesus' lips. Here we see one of those lessons that was apparently the most difficult to learn. The apostles were perfectly willing to suffer pain and persecution for the name of Jesus because it meant that they were functioning as Jesus' representatives. Nothing could have been more precious to them. But as Luke shows us throughout his works, that role was not at all limited to the apostles.

That was something of an ego-blow for them! Of course, it's only a blow to your ego if you look at it from the wrong perspective. If you're looking at the fact that your role is not unique, you might be disappointed, but if you're looking at the one you've been called to represent, the honor of the position will tend to dispel any petty disillusionment.

Representatives Of The Kingdom

Though Christians today are very familiar with the phrase "in the name of Jesus" we have often failed to understand it in the sense described above. Yet, from both the political/commercial context and the biblical use of the phrase, this meaning seems perfectly clear: to do anything "in the name of" someone is to do it as a representative of that person.

The only potential objection here is that, as I said, the phrase "in the name of" had a consistent usage in both commercial and political contexts of the first century. But are we really justified in applying the meaning of the phrase in *those* contexts to *these* passages? After all, Jesus isn't selling anything, so this isn't a commercial sort of thing. And, he's not a political figure, so this isn't about politics...or is it?

Actually, it is. Let's look at the final bit of text from the passage that started this whole thing:

> And they went on to another village. As they were going along the road, someone said to Him, "I will follow You wherever You go." And Jesus said to him, "The foxes have holes and the birds of the air have nests, but the Son of Man has nowhere to lay His head." And He said to another, "Follow Me." But he said, "Lord, permit me first to go and bury my father." But He said to him, "Allow the dead to bury their own dead; but as for you, go and proclaim everywhere the kingdom of God." Another also said, "I will follow You, Lord; but

first permit me to say good-bye to those at home." But Jesus said to him, "No one, after putting his hand to the plow and looking back, is fit for the kingdom of God."

(Luke 9:56-62)

Twice here at the conclusion of the passage Jesus refers to the Kingdom of God. These references, along with the accompanying title "Lord" which was used to address Jesus here, serve to ground the phrase "in the name of Jesus" in a political context. Consequently, there is no reason whatsoever to read this phrase in any way other than was common to the culture of the day. "In the name of Jesus" means nothing more complicated than "as a representative of Jesus." Simple…but profound almost beyond our ability to comprehend.

If this idea of representing Jesus had been presented to us for the first time in the New Testament, it would still be earth-shaking. However, the truth is that the true significance of "in the name of Jesus" is only a reiteration of a theme we would have already encountered a thousand times in the Bible, if only we'd been looking.

In fact, it is so important a theme that we find it on the very first page of the Bible!

SIX

The Heavenly Kingdom

It seems that at least once a year, while I'm standing in a checkout line, I see a tabloid with a headline that says something like, "Hubble Space Telescope Discovers Heaven!" This headline is usually accompanied by an "artist's rendition" of the discovery (the actual photograph is presumably classified). In the picture, we see what appears to be a large gleaming city of gold attached to a rocky, asteroid-like foundation.

Of course we laugh and roll our eyes. Who believes that heaven is a literal floating city? Who believes heaven is a physical place at all? Heaven can't be spied by a telescope. It's not "out there" somewhere waiting to be stumbled upon by intrepid space explorers.

I am always amused by tabloid articles like that. To be honest, I usually buy them, read the article and keep it in a file for future use. What attracts my attention the most, however, isn't just the silliness of the whole thing. What I find intriguing about such articles is the way that they demonstrate fundamental misunderstandings of the Biblical teaching on heaven. Unfortunately, these are not misunderstandings that only the non-Christian world has. Many mature Christians have a picture of our final destiny that is utterly out of keeping with the clear teaching of Scripture.

A few years ago I was speaking at a Jr. High youth conference. During the afternoon, we had set up elective seminars from which the students could choose. I offered a seminar called "Tough Questions." I told students they could come and ask any question they wanted to about God, the Bible, Christianity, other religions, etc. I didn't promise to be able to answer any and every question that was asked, of course, but I did promise to be able to help them at least begin thinking about how to find the answer. I also promised to suggest some resources to which they could turn. Generally, a Tough Questions seminar involves a lot of questions like: How did we get the Bible? Is Jesus really the only way? What about people who never hear about Jesus? Is suicide the unforgivable sin? On this particular Saturday afternoon, however, the questions took an unexpected direction. A definite theme developed that I hadn't really encountered before.

The seminar was only scheduled for an hour, and the room was very hot and close, so I told the 300 students packed into this little room that we would definitely finish things on schedule. After an hour, however, the questions were still coming fast and furious, so I told everyone that I would close things up for those who wanted to leave, but I would stick around if anyone wanted to stay. Over a hundred students stayed!

As the one hour seminar approached its fourth hour I turned the tables a bit. "Listen, guys," I said. "You've been asking me questions for almost three hours. Now its my turn. Let me ask you a question. It seems like an awful lot of these questions have to do with a common theme: heaven. We've talked about who will be there. We've talked about what we'll do. We've talked about what it will look like. We've even talked about whether we'll be able to understand everything there. Here's my question: What's with all the questions about heaven? Why the fascination?"

The room was silent.

No one said a word. I waited. Still no one said a word. So, I waited longer. Finally, this young girl stepped up to the plate. "Well," she said hesitantly, "please don't think I'm bad or something. I know that heaven's gonna be great. I know the angel band is gonna be kickin', so the worship will be awesome and everything, but...well, it just seems like after a thousand years or so of that it might get kind of..."

She wouldn't finish the sentence, so I filled in the blank. "Boring?" I asked. Just about every head in the room began to nod vigorously...and I despaired.

Historically, one of the greatest motivators for Christian faith and living has been the promise of heaven, but something has happened. While heaven certainly remains more attractive than the alternative, it no longer affects us the way it once did. It no longer motivates. It no longer inspires.

Some will argue, and they may be correct to some extent, that this is because we have become a culture of the *now*. When the present was difficult and painful, as was often the case before the technological revolution, future promises had great motivational power. We were *anxious* to look beyond the present to a more peaceful future existence. But now, when technology has made life so much easier, the present is no longer so painful and promises of future relief lose their edge.

I'm sure this is true to some extent, but I'm also convinced that much of the problem lies in the fact that our descriptions of heaven have become pathetic panderings. The common Christian conception of heaven today often resonates more with ancient pagan mythology and tabloid journalism than with Biblical teaching.

Debunking The Myths

Ask anyone in the West, Christian or non-Christian, and you will get basically the same description of heaven. There will be streets of gold. There will be pearly gates. There will be a glassy sea and harp music and angels. It will be beautiful and perfect.

Ask what we will do there, however, and the answers get vague. Non-Christians are prone to say that we will do whatever we want, that heaven is the state of finally being free to do all the things you haven't been able to do in this life. Christians, on the other hand, will generally say that we will worship God. Twenty-four hours a day for the rest of eternity, we will sit around the throne and sing God's praise.

J.I. Packer has articulated what many Christians feel: "When I was young," he said, "I was afraid of both heaven and hell. Hell because it sounded awful and heaven because it sounded dull."

Of course, the angel band will surely be kickin' and the worship will be awesome. But I confess that I too am afraid that, after a thousand years or so, it might get a little...well, boring.

Now some will say that this is only because I haven't experienced true, pure worship and that this will be like a sweet nectar of which I cannot imbibe enough. That may be true, but my concern is more practical than that. The fact is that this is not precisely what the Bible teaches our eternal destiny will consist of.

When most people describe heaven as they believe the Bible teaches it, their descriptions never stray beyond the New Jerusalem. While scattered throughout the book of Revelation to some extent, the descriptions of this city are concentrated in chapter 21. There John tells us:

And he carried me away in the Spirit to a great and high mountain, and showed me the holy city, Jerusalem, coming down out of heaven from God, having the glory of God. Her brilliance was like a very costly stone, as a stone of crystal-clear jasper. It had a great and high wall, with twelve gates, and at the gates twelve angels; and names were written on them, which are the names of the twelve tribes of the sons of Israel. There were three gates on the east and three gates on the north and three gates on the south and three gates on the west. And the wall of the city had twelve foundation stones, and on them were the twelve names of the twelve apostles of the Lamb. The one who spoke with me had a gold measuring rod to measure the city, and its gates and its wall. The city is laid out as a square, and its length is as great as the width; and he measured the city with the rod, fifteen hundred miles; its length and width and height are equal. And he measured its wall, seventy-two yards, according to human measurements, which are also angelic measurements. The material of the wall was jasper; and the city was pure gold, like clear glass. The foundation stones of the city wall were adorned with every kind of precious stone. The first foundation stone was jasper; the second, sapphire; the third, chalcedony; the fourth, emerald; the fifth, sardonyx; the sixth, sardius; the seventh, chrysolite; the eighth, beryl; the ninth, topaz; the tenth, chrysoprase; the eleventh, jacinth; the twelfth, amethyst. And the twelve gates were twelve pearls; each one of the gates was a single pearl. And the street of the city was pure gold, like transparent glass. I saw no temple in it, for the Lord God the Almighty and the Lamb are its temple. And the city has no need of the sun or of the moon to shine on it, for the glory of God has illumined it, and its lamp is the Lamb.

(Revelation 21:10-23)

This passage summarizes the average Christian's conception of heaven. It's all there! Golden streets, pearly gates, the light of God's presence. But this is not the whole picture. Often overlooked are the verses that introduce this passage:

Then I saw a new heaven and a new earth; for the first heaven and the first earth passed away, and there is no longer any sea. And I saw the holy city, new Jerusalem, coming down out of heaven from God, made ready as a bride adorned for her husband.

(Revelation 21:1-2)

The final reality which was shown to John in this vision involved both a new heaven and a new...*earth*. It was this new earth on which the heavenly city came to rest.

And those gates of pearl? Check this out:

The nations will walk by its light [the lamp of the Lamb, God's glory] and the kings of the earth will bring their glory into it. In the daytime (for there will be no night there) *its gates will never be closed*; and they will bring the glory and the honor of the nations into it;

(Revelation 21:23-26)

In these verses, we find a statement that is very difficult to incorporate into our common conceptions of heaven. How can there be kings? Kings imply kingdoms and kingdoms imply activities that are utterly incongruent with our picture of heaven as a 24/7 praise and worship service.

But John saw quite clearly that there would be kings. How can that be? I have heard people try to argue that the kings in view here are pagan rulers finally forced to bow in submission to the King of kings before facing the final judgment, but such an argument has no force. The chronology of the book of Revelation is difficult to discern at times, but there can be no doubt that chapter 21 describes events that are to take place *after* the final judgment. Whoever these kings are who continually bring their treasures before God, they have to be believers. If nothing else, the last verse of chapter 21 makes this abundantly clear:

> ...and nothing unclean, and no one who practices abomination and lying, shall ever come into it, but only those whose names are written in the Lamb's book of life.
>
> (Revelation 21:27)

These are Christian kings and they rule nations populated by the redeemed followers of Jesus Christ. But, of course, there cannot be kings and kingdoms unless life in heaven is played out on a far grander scale than most of us imagine. Our typical conception of heaven as an endless gathering of singers around the holy throne does not leave room for the fullness of the Bible's teaching on eternity.

Part of the problem, of course, arises from the fact that the word "heaven" is a very confusing word. We use it to mean all sorts of things. A really good meal is "heaven." When some great honor or pleasure is bestowed on us, we're said to be "in heaven." And, of course, we pray to "God in heaven" and ask "who have I in heaven but you Jesus?" But the Bible also speaks about "against the spiritual forces of wickedness in the heavenly places." (Ephesians 6:12).

Now, many translations render this passage from Ephesians as the NAB does, "spiritual forces of darkness in the *heavenly places*", but the Greek word is literally "heavens." This underscores the difficulty we have in speaking about heaven. The meanings of this word vary, both in popular speech and in biblical teaching.

Biblical Meanings Of "The Heavens"

Interestingly, both the Greek and Hebrew words we usually translate as "heaven" are plural. Literally, they are "the heavens." They are used in several ways:

First, as part of a *merismus*. A merismus is a figure of speech in which two opposite extremes of a category are mentioned as a reference to the whole of the category. When we say someone is praying "day and night" we mean that they are praying around the clock. Perhaps the most common merismus, though, both in the Bible and in our own culture, is the phrase "heaven and earth." If someone is said to be willing to move "heaven and earth" to accomplish something, we simply mean that they are willing to move all obstacles. When the Bible says that God created the "heavens and the earth," we simply mean that He created everything; that is, that "all things came into being through Him, and apart from Him nothing came into being that has come into being" (John 1:3). Similarly, when the Bible says that John was given a vision of a "new heaven and a new earth," what is being communicated is that *all* of reality is to be made new again. In fact, that is precisely what the book of Revelation tells us: "And He who sits on the throne said, 'Behold, I am making *all things* new.'" (Revelation 21:5a)

Second, these terms are used as a reference to the *sky*. The word "heavens" is often used in the Bible, just as in our own culture, to refer to the skies...and beyond. When we talk about the "stars in the heavens" we aren't referring to a spiritual reality, but to what we see in the sky at night. This use of the word is a direct carry-over from the Bible where the word often refers to physical reality beyond the earth's surface:

> Then God said, "Let there be lights in the expanse of the heavens to separate the day from the night, and let them be for signs and for seasons and for days and years; and let them be for lights in the expanse of the heavens to give light on the earth"; and it was so." God made the two great lights, the greater light to govern the day, and the lesser light to govern the night; He made the stars also. God placed them in the expanse of the heavens to give light on the earth, and to govern the day and the night, and to separate the light from the darkness; and God saw that it was good.
>
> (Genesis 1:14-18)

> Therefore there was born even of one man, and him as good as dead at that, as many descendants AS THE STARS OF HEAVEN IN NUMBER, AND INNUMERABLE AS THE SAND WHICH IS BY THE SEASHORE.
>
> (Hebrews 11:12)

Third, these words are used as a reference to *spiritual reality*. Also common in the Bible is the use of the word "heavens" to refer to the realm of spirit activity. This includes evil spirits, Satan and those fallen angels whom he commands, which are often referred to as "powers":

> "But in those days, after that tribulation, THE SUN WILL BE DARKENED AND THE MOON WILL NOT GIVE ITS LIGHT, AND THE STARS WILL BE FALLING from heaven, and the powers that are in the heavens will be shaken. Then they will see THE SON OF MAN COMING IN CLOUDS with great power and glory."
>
> (Mark 13:24-26)

> For our struggle is not against flesh and blood, but against the rulers, against the powers, against the world forces of this darkness, against the spiritual forces of wickedness in the heavenly places.
>
> (Ephesians 6:12)

Spiritual forces of good are also said to operate from "the heavens":

> And suddenly there appeared with the angel a multitude of the heavenly host praising God and saying, "Glory to God in the highest, and on earth peace among men with whom He is pleased." When the angels had gone away from them into heaven, the shepherds began saying to one another, "Let us go straight to Bethlehem

then, and see this thing that has happened which the Lord has made known to us."

(Luke 2:13-15)

But even if we, or an angel from heaven, should preach to you a gospel contrary to what we have preached to you, he is to be accursed!

(Galatians 1:8)

And, of course, God is said to exist in, and extend his power from, the heavens:

Then Jehoshaphat stood in the assembly of Judah and Jerusalem, in the house of the LORD before the new court, and he said, "O LORD, the God of our fathers, are You not God in the heavens? And are You not ruler over all the kingdoms of the nations? Power and might are in Your hand so that no one can stand against You."

(2 Chronicles 20:5-6)

Why should the nations say, "Where, now, is their God?" But our God is in the heavens; He does whatever He pleases."

(Psalm 115:2-3)

For the wrath of God is revealed from heaven against all ungodliness and unrighteousness of men who suppress the truth in unrighteousness.

(Romans 1:18)

So, "heavens" is often a general purpose word used to refer to spiritual, as opposed to strictly physical, reality. As such, it is sometimes the word used when speaking of the present dwelling place of human spirits that have been separated from their bodies at death:

> "And then He will send forth the angels, and will gather together His elect from the four winds, from the farthest end of the earth to the farthest end of heaven."
>
> (Mark 13:27)

Here we see the idea that, at Jesus return, he will gather all of his followers, whether still alive (from the farthest end of earth) or dead (to the farthest end of heaven).

Now, this notion fits in perfectly with the way we typically speak of Christians who have died. We usually say that they are in "heaven" with Jesus. And, in one sense, this is true. As spirits, they exist presently in the realm of spiritual reality, rather than physical reality. Just as Jesus promised the thief on the cross that they would be together in paradise that very day, departed Christian souls exist now in a disembodied state in the presence of God.

This is not, however, "heaven" in the sense that we use the term when referring to eternal life after the Millennium. Presently, departed believers live in the "heavens," but the final reality that awaits us...the final "heaven" if you will, is a very different proposition.

To begin with, eternal life will be lived out in a physical universe. Having resurrected believers to new physical[24] bodies

---

[24] Although, of course, not physical bodies of exactly the same sort as we have now. Jesus' own resurrection body is the model of what our new bodies will be like (cf. 1Co 15:20-23).

God will usher us into unending, glorious life in the new heaven and the new earth (i.e. all of reality). This will be a physical place, of which the gold-bricked, pearly-gated New Jerusalem will be but a part.

What will we do for eternity?

No Plan "B"

We will do what we were made to do in the first place: we will represent God in creation. This was God's initial plan for us and it remains his central purpose for human existence. God does not have Plan B's. When Adam and Eve sinned, God did not say "Okay now, don't panic...we can still work with this! I'll just downgrade my expectations a bit and revise the plan."

No. God has never given up on us or on the purpose for which we were designed. We were made to represent God in creation and represent God in creation we shall. The entire span of history between the Fall and the Second Coming is a mere wrinkle that God is ironing out.

But what does it mean to "represent God in creation?" What will this look like?

On some levels, that question is impossible to answer. Life in the midst of the wrinkle makes it quite difficult to perceive what things were - or will be - like on either side. However, some insight is possible when we look at what God expected of Adam and Eve prior to their expulsion from the Garden.

God's intention for humanity to function as His regents was explicit from the moment of their creation. But what did He intend that regency to look like? We find some hint back in Genesis:

> God blessed them; and God said to them, "Be
> fruitful and multiply, and fill the earth, and

> subdue it; and rule over the fish of the sea and
> over the birds of the sky and over every living
> thing that moves on the earth."
>
> (Genesis 1:28)

There are five commands here, each one building upon the previous command: be fruitful and in your success at bearing children, fill up the earth so that there are enough of you to subdue it and in your subjugation of it, rule over it.

The commands to be fruitful, multiply and fill the earth require little or no explanation. These are easy enough to understand. The command to subdue the earth, on the other hand, is more complicated.

In English, subduing something means to bring it under control by force. The Hebrew word being translated here (kabash) has the same basic meaning. It is not a common word in Scripture, but where it occurs, this meaning is clear:

> Moses said to them, "If the sons of Gad and the
> sons of Reuben, everyone who is armed for
> battle, will cross with you over the Jordan in the
> presence of the LORD, and the land is subdued
> before you, then you shall give them the land of
> Gilead for a possession;"
>
> (Numbers 32:29)

> King David also dedicated these to the LORD,
> with the silver and gold that he had dedicated
> from all the nations which he had subdued;
>
> (2 Samuel 8:11)

Now, the use of this term in regard to hostile foreign nations is perfectly understandable. Such nations were in opposition to God and His people and so the use of force was necessary to bring them under control. But in what sense was the creation out of control so that it needed to be subdued? Remember, this command was given prior to the Fall and there is no hint of a prophetic element in it. The command was apparently applicable to creation even before human sin plunged the natural world into chaos. But how can that be?

A few years ago, I watched an episode of the popular cartoon sitcom *The Simpsons*, in which Homer dreamt of being in the Garden of Eden. In Homer's dream, he lived in a state of perpetual pleasure. There were dessert-bushes with succulent apple pies just waiting to be plucked. Pigs wandered around offering pork-chops and bacon...all of which could be obtained without harm to the animals themselves. It was more than perfect. It was bliss.

I suspect that most Christians today have something like this in mind when they think of the Garden of Eden. We wouldn't quite couch it in these precise terms, of course, but something similar to Homer's vision lurks in the back of our minds.

Perhaps the most central feature of life in the Garden, according to popular conception, was leisure. Whatever else might or might not have been present, the one thing certain to have been missing from the Garden was work. After all, hard work was a curse that came as a consequence of the Fall, right?

Wrong.

The curse pronounced on Adam after his sin was not that of work, but of *futility*:

> Then to Adam He said, "Because you have listened to the voice of your wife, and have eaten from the tree about which I commanded you, saying, 'You shall not eat from it'; cursed is the ground because of you; in toil you will eat of it, all the days of your life. Both thorns and

> thistles it shall grow for you; and you will eat
> the plants of the field; by the sweat of your face
> you will eat bread, till you return to the ground,
> because from it you were taken; for you are
> dust, and to dust you shall return."
>
> (Genesis 3:17-19)

Because of sin, we are cursed to work hard and have nothing
to show for it. We plow the ground and plant grain, but thorns
and thistles try to choke it out. We build things and they fall
apart. Whenever I am speaking to students on this subject I ask
if any of them have ever lost a paper when the computer
crashed. When just about everyone raises their hands, I tell
them that Adam and Eve never lost their term papers...their
hard-drives never crashed. The constant frustration of working
hard only to have little or nothing to show for it became part of
the human experience at the Fall, not before.

Hard work is not a curse. We were designed to work hard, as
the command to "subdue" creation implies. To subdue anything
requires hard work, serious effort...even, dare I say it?...*sweat.*
To most Christians, the idea of sweaty effort in the Garden of
Eden is unthinkable, but this is because our conception of Eden
is taken more from silly sitcoms than from God's Word. When
we look to Scripture, we see that the very first orders given by
God to His regents in creation were that they fill up the earth
and bring it under control.

But what effort was needed? Wasn't the earth perfect before
the Fall?

Perfection

The answer to that question depends entirely on what you
mean by "perfect." There are two senses in which we use the
word. The first sense is of lacking blemish or wrongness. An

apple could be described as "perfect" if there are no bruises and it is shaped just the way an apple should be. The second sense, however, is of completeness. Someone who scores a 300 is said to have bowled a "perfect" game. We don't mean by this that every throw was necessarily without error of any kind, but that the score was all it could possibly be. The rules of the game don't allow for a higher score. This sense of perfection as completeness is the one most often found in Scripture:

> For we know in part and we prophesy in part; but when the perfect comes, the partial will be done away.
>
> (1 Corinthians 13:9-10)

In this verse, we clearly see the connection between perfection and completeness. To know or prophesy "in part" does not mean that we do so with error and imperfection, but that such knowledge or prophesy does not encompass all knowledge, for much still remains unknown or undisclosed.

Interestingly, in his letter to the Philippians, Paul included a passage that contrasts both of these different uses of "perfect":

> Not that I have…already become *perfect*, but I press on so that I may lay hold of that for which also I was laid hold of by Christ Jesus. Brethren, I do not regard myself as having laid hold of it yet; but one thing I do: forgetting what lies behind and reaching forward to what lies ahead, I press on toward the goal for the prize of the upward call of God in Christ Jesus. Let us therefore, *as many as are perfect*, have this attitude; and if in anything you have a different attitude, God will reveal that also to you;

(Philippians 3:12-15)

Here, the first use of "perfect" is in the sense of "without blemish." Paul is indicating that he does not consider himself to be without error or imperfection. And yet, just a few words later, he identifies himself as one who is "perfect." This second use, however, refers to the fact that through Jesus, God has made Paul fully human; complete in a way that can never be true of non-believers.

Something similar is in view when, in Matthew 5:48, we are told that Jesus commanded that we be "...perfect, as your Heavenly Father is perfect." This command has caused a great deal of debate, but I think it all unnecessary. Jesus was making neither a prophetic command that could only be fulfilled at some future date nor a rhetorical point intended to show us our inability to do what God requires of us on our own. Rather, Jesus was commanding that we be complete; that is, be everything that it is possible for us to be, given the present conditions of life. Odd as it may sound to us, perfection in the biblical sense can be achieved in *stages*. An artist may step back from a sculpture and remark of the mouth, "perfect," while still recognizing that a great deal of work remains to be done. In the same way, Jesus commands that we be everything that we can be, given the present circumstances and the work that has already been done by God on our behalf.

Only when we understand perfection in this broader, biblical sense, can we begin to imagine what was being asked of Adam and Eve. If, by perfect, we mean that the world was without blemish before the Fall, then we would be entirely correct. However, if by perfect we mean that there were no possible improvements that could be made, then we would be wrong. God apparently envisioned a creation which glorified Him to an ever-increasing extent and he assigned human beings the task of bringing this vision to fruition.

Culture And Cultivation

It is impossible to say what, precisely, this task would have looked like - or will look like again someday - simply because the context in which such work was carried out was so radically different from the one in which we presently exist. At best, we can imagine such work in broad outlines. Most basically, I believe that our role of ruling and subduing creation was intended to be carried out by care and cultivation.

By care I simply mean that we were made to be stewards over creation, providing for the well-being of it and its inhabitants. By cultivation, I mean that we were intended to shape the basic materials of creation into new forms. We were meant to plow rows and plant food. We were meant to build roads and cities. We were meant to create art, poetry and music. By these tasks, we represent in creation the God who is endlessly caring and creative and who made us as His Image. This, I believe Scripture teaches, is that for which we are made and that to which believers will be restored in the end.

The Heavenly Frigidaire

It is impossible to over-grandeurize the gloriousness of the scene John described in Revelation 21: "and the kings of the earth will bring their glory into it [the heavenly city]." Can you imagine?

When I see this scene described, as corny as this may sound, what I picture is a giant refrigerator set beside the throne in the New Jerusalem. Remember when you were young and you painted a picture, or wrote a poem or did well on a test? When you brought it home, what did your Mom do with it? Where does one display such a "treasure?" On the refrigerator, of course! And up it went, stuck there with a magnet for all to see. When I read of the kings of the earth continually coming in, bringing their "glory" into the heavenly city, I cannot help but think of a similar scene taking place, over and over again throughout eternity.

Forget the questions and the paradoxical puzzles we thought would be solved if only we could ask Him face to face. There at the foot of the throne, with the throngs of angels gathered round and watching intently, our questions will slip quickly from our minds and hide themselves behind our awe. Nothing that we think important to ask now will even be remembered in those moments. All that we will be able to say is, "Lord, I...well, I did this for you. Here."

And God, leaping to His feet with flashing eyes will exclaim "Marvelous! This...you did this for Me? Really?"

Swallow hard. "Yes. For You!"

And He will examine our offering, whatever it may be, a poem or a picture, a song or a new road between cities...perhaps a chart of the stars in the new heaven or a study of the biology of redeemed flesh or a history of the Millennium...whatever it is, He will examine it with an intensity of which we cannot conceive. And then...oh, and then, He will turn to us and smile, an expression that will utterly unmake us for the joy of it, and He will declare to the watching multitudes, "Do you see this? For Me...she did this for Me!" And then He will say "You know where this is going? Right here!" And with a resounding thwack, He will stick it high on the Heavenly Frigidaire.

Perhaps then He will look at us again with sparkling eyes and ask, "Do you have anything else?"

"Well," you'll say, "I *do* have this one thing that I was thinking about getting started on, but it would take, like, a thousand years to get done...oh, right...I'll be back!"

Can you imagine?

Of course you can't. Our present reality is so afflicted by the horror of sin, death and decay, that to grasp some true perception of the life that awaits us is beyond our ability. The important thing to remember is that what awaits us is *life*...real living, not endless millennia of stupefying rest and relaxation. Not 24/7 praise and worship services for all eternity. Of course there will be praise and of course the angel band will be kickin'...but we were not made to literally sing without ceasing. There are some angels who were apparently made for that very purpose and they will thus find joy and meaning in fulfilling their destiny. But that is not *our* destiny as the Bible predicts it. Our eternal destiny is to return to doing the very thing we were made to do in the first place: bringing God glory by representing Him, mediating His presence to every corner of creation.

We cannot know exactly what our eternal life with God will look like. I suspect something like I have described above will play a part, but the reality will undoubtedly be larger, bolder and more wonderful by far.

This is the heaven. This is the promise of eternal life which is held before us, drawing us on through the oft-gloomy days of life in the here and now.

SEVEN

Kingdoms In Conflict

The air was still and every restless movement from the crowd reverberated off the stone walls. Dust caught in the backs of their throats, but everyone did the best they could to stifle the coughs that demanded to be let out. Occasionally, one escaped, sounding like an explosion in the close quarters of the synagogue.

Every eye was on the man who slowly made his way to the front of the room. Silently, he reached for one of the scrolls and unrolled it. He scanned its contents with the practiced eye of one long-familiar with the Holy Words. Finding his place, he looked up at the expectant crowd and smiled.

Unconsciously, everyone leaned forward, anxious to hear every word spoken by this remarkable young man, this teacher from Nazareth. Laying as it did on the Via Maris, the trade route between the Mediterranean and Damascus, Capernaum saw its fair share of interesting visitors, but none quite so intriguing as this Jesus fellow.

What would he say? What passage from the Scriptures would he read this Sabbath day? Everyone waited with breathless anticipation.

Finally, Jesus began to speak. As he read the Scriptures and explained them, people listened, enraptured. After a while, unable to contain themselves, they began looking at one another, eyes wide in amazement. Some whispered to their seat-mates.

"What is this?" they asked. "He doesn't sound like one of the scribes at all. He teaches as though he has authority. Who is he?"

Suddenly, Jesus' teaching and the quiet whispering of his audience was shattered by a loud cry. Everyone started and whirled around to find the source of this shocking interruption. Jesus fell silent.

A man who looked like he hadn't bathed in a month of Sabbaths was waving unsteadily on his feet, his eyes bloodshot and watery.

"What business do we have with each other, Jesus of Nazareth?" he cried, his voice loud and broken. "Have you come to destroy us?"

The crowd in the synagogue looked at one another with wide eyes. Sharp whispers of "unclean spirit" and "demon" could be heard racing through the crowd.

The man ignored them all. "I know who you are," he spat, staring at Jesus. "You're the Holy One of God." Somehow, the word "holy" sounded like something that made him want to vomit.

The man fell silent and glared through hate-filled eyes at the teacher in the front of the synagogue. Everyone looked to see Jesus' reaction, but there was little to observe. Jesus sat quietly on the stool, his hands clasped loosely in his lap, his eyes fixed steadily on his accuser.

Ever so subtly, Jesus shook his head. "Be quiet," he said softly but firmly. "Be quiet and come out of him."

The men of the synagogue frowned in puzzlement. What kind of response was this? Didn't Jesus understand what he was dealing with here? An unclean spirit...the man was under the control of a demonic entity! This was serious business!

Drastic measures were called for! At the very least, he needed to...

Their thoughts were interrupted by a commotion behind them. They whirled back around in time to see the man fall to the ground, his body convulsing violently. He screamed once, an ear-splitting, soul-shivering sound that caused many to throw their hands up and cover their ears.

Then, as suddenly as it had started, it was over. The scream was cut off sharply and the convulsions ended. The synagogue grew silent as a tomb. No one dared to move an inch or speak a word.

The man lay on the dusty stone floor as though dead, but after a moment, he opened his eyes. They were clear! Slowly, he sat up, shaking his head as though to clear away cobwebs from some unimaginably deep, drugged sleep.

Everyone held their breath and watched as the man looked around the room. His eyes came to rest on Jesus. He smiled, and his eyes grew watery again. This time, though, it was tears of joy and relief that clouded his vision. Jesus smiled back and nodded slightly.

The room went wild! Everyone was talking at once. Some were exclaiming to one another while some shouted questions at Jesus.

Towards the front of the room, an old man stood to his feet. He began clapping his gnarled hands, calling the younger men around him to order. Gradually the room quieted. The elder looked at Jesus for a long moment before turning back to the crowd.

"What is this?" he asked. "A new teaching, and with authority. He commands even the unclean spirits...and they obey him!"

Evil Spirits In The Modern Worldview

This is the scene described to us in Mark 1:21-27. It is very difficult for us, as modern readers, to understand the significance of such an event.

To begin with, we're not sure what to do with the whole notion of demonic spirits. Most evangelical Christians accept the existence of such beings on faith, since the Bible speaks of them frequently. An intellectual acknowledgement of their existence, however, is hardly sufficient preparation to deal with a story such as this.

We may acknowledge the existence of evil spirits in theory, but in practice, it seems that most Christians make one of two mistakes regarding them. One mistake is to virtually ignore them. The other mistake is to give them more credit than they deserve.

The first mistake is easy to make in a culture such as ours. Our preoccupation with all things scientific leads us to attribute everything that happens, from sickness to disaster, to natural causes. In our culture, belief in demonic spirits seems primitive and superstitious, akin to belief in Santa Clause. Let's be honest, many of us read the biblical stories that talk about people being afflicted by demons and think, at least privately, that we're probably reading an ignorant description of a schizophrenic or some other psychological malady. We may not think in exactly those terms, but on some level, many of us dismiss some of the Bible's descriptions of demonic activity as the words of ignorant primitives faced with a situation they simply didn't understand.

If you find that you're inclined to think this way, it is worth noting that the Bible does not attribute *all* illness, either physical or psychological, to demons. The biblical writers were well-aware that some diseases and ailments were the result of natural causes. Some were inherited, some were acquired later in life. It's that temporal snobbery again, to think that belief in demonic spirits was simply due to ignorance about physiology and psychology. True, many people in earlier times incorrectly attributed certain conditions to demons[25], but this does not mean that ancient people thought that *all* dysfunction was the result of spirit involvement. If you read the Bible carefully, you will see a sophisticated distinction between illnesses with a natural cause and illnesses with a supernatural cause.

The Bible in no way attributes every illness to demons. It simply acknowledges that such beings are real and that they do have a significant influence on human life.

This is, of course, not an exclusively Biblical concept. Just about every human culture that has ever existed has had some belief in spirits of this sort.

For the last several years, our church has spent time during the summer doing short-term missions work in native villages in the Alaskan bush. Among the Eskimo, Athabaskan and Aleut people there, we have frequently encountered stories and belief in spirit beings known, in one dialect, as the Ilikchik...the Little People. These are spirits that supposedly enjoy frightening and hurting the natives whenever possible. In certain parts of Alaska, just about everyone has stories about encounters with these creatures that will cause your hair to stand on end. These are not just the Alaskan equivalent of urban legends. In some parts of Alaska (tellingly, the parts with the least exposure to the gospel) the people live in genuine fear of these spirits. When I first heard some of these stories, my first thought was that these sounded an awfully lot like demons. I was reluctant, however, to pass that judgment until speaking with some native Christian believers. When I did so, I found

---

[25] As when medieval physicians sometimes tried to cure mental illnesses by drilling holes in the patients heads to let out the demons.

that mature Christians there have no hesitation in calling the Ilikchik precisely what they are: demonic spirits.

Such stories are not limited to Alaska, of course. Everywhere you go in the world, you will find a belief in similar type of creatures. Of course, they all have different names. The word demon is from the Greek. The Hebrews called them Shedim. In Japan, they are called the Yokai. In South America, they are commonly referred to as Yoshi. Muslims refer to these beings by several names, including Jinn and Afrit.

The question is, why should so many different cultures have similar beliefs in such beings? One possible answer, of course, is simply that such spirits are real. Now, as Christians, we can and should be discerning and ready to discard the many myths and legends that grow up around such spirits. However, it is important that we not throw out belief in the existence of such beings with the many false teachings that surround them. The Bible clearly acknowledges their existence and involvement in human affairs[26].

The second mistake that Christians are likely to make is to give demonic spirits too much credit. Some Christians seem to think that every sniffle and tic is proof positive of the operation of evil spiritual forces. Every psychological issue, from depression to schizophrenia, is attributed to the activity of a demonic spirit. Trouble sleeping? Demon! Sleeping too much? Demon! Hungry all the time? Demon. I actually have in my possession a book entitled *Help, Lord - The Devil Wants Me Fat!*[27] Now, that may be the case, but I think most people

---

[26] While the Bible does not have a great deal to say about the origins and nature of demonic spirits, most theologians believe from Scripture that demons are fallen angels; i.e. those angelic beings which sided with Satan and were cast out of the God's presence 2 Pet. 2:4, Rev. 12:4.

[27] C.S. Lovett, *Help, Lord - The Devil Wants Me Fat!* (Baldwin Park: Personal Christianity, 1977).

will agree with me that an addiction to snack foods should not be automatically blamed on demonic activity.

It seems to me that fewer people make this second kind of mistake than make the first, but it is not at all unusual to encounter someone who seems to think there's a demon lurking behind all things negative. Actually, many people don't just see demons everywhere...they see Satan himself everywhere. For some, Satan has become a being of almost limitless power, sort of an evil god who possesses the attributes of omnipresence, omnipotence and omniscience.

Of course, Satan, that archangel who led the rebellion against God and was cast out of God's presence, has none of these attributes. He may have some grand and horrific schemes, but his ability to carry them out is severely circumscribed, in part because of his own finite power and in part because God Himself exercises sovereign control over him.

Evil Spirits And The Ancient World

This brings us back, finally, to the scene which began this chapter. Recall the question that was raised when Jesus cast out the demonic spirit afflicting the poor man in the synagogue: "What is this?" the crowd asked. "A new teaching, and with authority. He commands even the unclean spirits...and they obey him!"

The Jewish people, of course, knew something about demons. They even knew something about dealing with them. Jewish exorcisms, however, were apparently elaborate affairs lasting a considerable period of time with no real guarantee of lasting success[28]. In light of this, Jesus' exorcism was startling. He said "leave" and the demons left. No special words, no

---

[28] For examples of the type of thing which constituted Jewish exorcism, see the Talmud: Schabbath, xiv, 3; Aboda Zara, xii, 2; Sanhedrin, x, 1.

props, no elaborate rituals[29]. He just uttered the command to go and they were gone.

Interestingly, there is an intimate connection between Jesus' authority over evil spirits and his announcement of the Kingdom. We have alluded to this briefly in a previous chapter, but the time has come to unpack this important observation.

On several occasions, Jesus described his casting out of demons as proof that the Kingdom of God was present:

> Summoning two of his disciples, John sent them to the Lord, saying, "Are You the Expected One, or do we look for someone else?" When the men came to Him, they said, "John the Baptist has sent us to You, to ask, 'Are You the Expected One, or do we look for someone else?' At that very time He cured many people of diseases and afflictions *and evil spirits;* and He gave sight to many who were blind. And He answered and said to them, "Go and report to John what you have seen and heard: the BLIND RECEIVE SIGHT, the lame walk, the lepers are cleansed, and the deaf hear, the dead are raised up, the POOR HAVE THE GOSPEL PREACHED TO THEM."
>
> (Luke 7:19-22)

> And He called the twelve together, and *gave them power and authority over all the demons* and to heal diseases. And He sent them out to

---

[29] For instance, the Jewish historian Josephus tells of one Jewish exorcist who supposedly made use of a ring constructed according to some long-lost procedure invented by Solomon (Antiq. viii, ii5).

proclaim the kingdom of God and to perform healing.

(Luke 9:1-2)

These types of connections can be found in many passages throughout the Gospels. The question, of course, is why? Why did Jesus see his authority over demons as being so intimately connected to his proclamation of the Kingdom of God?

The Dark Kingdom

It is only possible to answer that question when we remember that God's Kingdom is not the only spiritual kingdom discussed in Scripture. Throughout the Bible, though most pointedly in the New Testament, we find descriptions of another kingdom: the kingdom of darkness.

Now, the actual phrase "kingdom of darkness" is never used in the Bible. However, this is probably an attempt to avoid the misconception that the Kingdom of God and the kingdom of darkness are somehow equal but opposites. So, while this precise phrase does not occur, the activity of Satan and the demonic spirits under his control are frequently described as emanating from an evil *kingdom*:

> For He rescued us from the domain of darkness, and transferred us to the Kingdom of His beloved Son...
>
> (Colossians 1:13)

Here, Christ's Kingdom is contrasted with an evil domain or, literally, *authority* to which fallen humanity is apparently subject. Not only are Satan and his minions said to have some kind of authority over sinful humanity, but they are frequently described as actual *rulers*:

> And you were dead in your trespasses and sins, in which you formerly walked according to the course of this world, according to the prince of the power of the air[30], of the spirit that is now working in the sons of disobedience.
>
> (Ephesians 2:1-2)

> For our struggle is not against flesh and blood, but against the rulers, against the powers, against the world forces of this darkness, against the spiritual forces of wickedness in the heavenly places.
>
> (Ephesians 6:12)

Neither is this notion of evil spirits as ruling over fallen humanity restricted to the New Testament. In Daniel, we find the following words of an angel, presumably Gabriel, giving us a rare glimpse into the spiritual reality that operates behind the scenes of everyday life:

> "But the prince of the kingdom of Persia was withstanding me for twenty-one days; then behold, Michael, one of the chief princes, came to help me, for I had been left there with the kings of Persia... Then he said, "Do you understand why I came to you? But I shall now return to fight against the prince of Persia; so I am going forth, and behold, the prince of Greece is about to come."

---

[30] A euphemism for Satan.

(Daniel 10:13, 20)

Satan is even called a god, not in the sense of having equal power or authority, but in the sense of having been permitted to exercise authority as a ruler over fallen humanity:

> ...the god of this world has blinded the minds of the unbelieving so that they might not see the light of the gospel of the glory of Christ, who is the image of God.
>
> (2 Corinthians 4:4)

What seems to have happened is this: When Adam and Eve sinned, they essentially cast their allegiance with Satan much as the fallen angels did. Consequently, God granted Satan the right to rule over us, at least for a time. This fact is made abundantly clear when we note Satan's attempt to steer Jesus off-track:

> Again, the devil took Him to a very high mountain and showed Him all the kingdoms of the world and their glory; and he said to Him, "All these things I will give You, if You fall down and worship me."
>
> (Matthew 4:8-9)

Given these references to a kingdom of darkness, the connection between casting out demons and announcing the Kingdom of God becomes clear. The Kingdom of God does not arrive in a vacuum. A spiritual kingdom already exists and exercises authority in human affairs. Therefore, the arrival of the Kingdom of God creates a conflict. These are what the many references to demonic outcries against Jesus' ministry demonstrate. These spirits recognized, or at the very least *suspected*, that Jesus' arrival signaled a political upheaval[31].

Delegated Authority

Now, if it were only Jesus who had this authority over evil spirits, then the conflict between Kingdoms would not appear to be too intense. What we would have would be something like a king making a royal visit to a foreign land. Because of who he is, the visiting king might be able to exercise a certain degree of authority over the country's citizens, but that would be as far as it goes.

However, Jesus did not just exercise authority over demons himself. He also delegated that authority to the twelve apostles (Lk. 9:1-2), which is perhaps not so surprising. In Luke 10:17, however, we see that this authority was also delegated to a much larger group of followers. According to Mark 16:17[32], the ability to exercise authority over demonic spirits was one of the basic signs accompanying faith in Christ.

The Preeminence Of The Incarnation

We have said that Israel, the incarnation and the Church are all manifestations of the Kingdom of God and this is true. However, this does not necessarily mean that they are all *equal*

---

[31]   That is, if spiritual kingdoms can be said to be "political." It is a bit of a stretch to use the word in this way, but I assume most readers will understand what I mean.

[32]   As most versions of the Bible note, the earliest and most reliable manuscripts do not have this portion of Mark. However, in this case, the notion of believers having authority over demonic spirits is well-attested throughout the New Testament. Mark 16:17 is quoted only because it provides the most explicit statement of this fact.

manifestations of it. We would be fools if we missed the fact that Christ's arrival signaled a new *kind* of manifestation, one imbued with tremendous power.

Christ's coming signaled a revolution in the power structure of the world. No longer did human beings need to be subject to the malicious whims of the evil spirits operating under the authority of their dark kingdom.

The Kingdom of God as manifest in Israel represented a *promise*. Israel existed as a sort of refuge, a safe-house if you will, in the midst of a world dominated by the kingdom of darkness.

The Kingdom of God as manifest in the incarnation, however, was the *fulfillment of that promise*. Jesus' arrival was no short-term mission, striking deep into enemy territory for a brief time so as to distribute help and hope to an oppressed people. Jesus' arrival signaled nothing short of a revolution, a radical overturning of the world order as it had stood from the time that Adam and Eve first turned from their true King, casting their allegiance with a false one.

If Israel was the promise of this coming revolution, then the Church is the *proclamation* of it. The Church exists to announce the reality of the Kingdom of God that has come near to us in the person of Christ.

A passage we have already looked at briefly, the second chapter of Ephesians, describes this perfectly. In addition to containing one of the most powerful statements you will find anywhere in Scripture – "by grace you have been saved" – this passage paints an important contrast. It is a contrast that is easily missed in the English translations, but if you look carefully, you will see it in any translation:

> And you were dead in your trespasses and sins,
> in which you formerly walked according to the

course of this world, according to the prince of the power of the air, of the spirit that is now working in the sons of disobedience. Among them we too all formerly lived in the lusts of our flesh, indulging the desires of the flesh and of the mind, and were by nature children of wrath, even as the rest. But God, being rich in mercy, because of His great love with which He loved us, even when we were dead in our transgressions, made us alive together with Christ (by grace you have been saved), and raised us up with Him, and seated us with Him in the heavenly places in Christ Jesus, so that in the ages to come He might show the surpassing riches of His grace in kindness toward us in Christ Jesus. For by grace you have been saved through faith; and that not of yourselves, it is the gift of God; not as a result of works, so that no one may boast. For we are His workmanship, created in Christ Jesus for good works, which God prepared beforehand so that we would walk in them.

(Ephesians 2:1-10)

Note the way that Paul describes all of us before we came to trust in Jesus:

1. We "walked around in" sin and transgression
2. We did what Satan wanted us to do

Not a good place to be, obviously, but because of His great love toward us, God has saved us, made us alive together with Christ, raised us up and seated us together with Christ in the heavenly places. The fact that Christ has been seated in "the heavenly places" is an indication of his position of power and authority over the spiritual realm. Since we are said to be "seated with him" there, then this is an indication that we have been delegated the same authority. What an amazing statement!

But perhaps more amazing still is the contrast that is painted between our old lives and our new lives as described in the second half of this passage. There we see that, in Christ:

1. We "walk around in" good deeds
2. We do what God wants us to do

Where formerly we "walked around in" deeds of sin and transgression, put before us by Satan, now in Christ we "walk around in" good deeds, prepared for us by God. "Walk around in" is a literal translation of a Greek phrase which means, essentially "to live lives characterized by…"

What Paul is describing here are kingdoms in conflict. The Kingdom of God is not the only game in town. There is another kingdom, a dark and insidious one, and life in that kingdom is characterized by rebellion, sin and transgression. Ironically, this kingdom is populated, not by oppressed masses, but by *defectors*. These are not just any defectors, of course, for as we have seen, human beings are created to be ambassadors of God Almighty. The citizenry of the kingdom of darkness is made up of renegade royalty, willing defectors from the Kingdom of God. Of course, the knowledge of our true nature, and our true citizenship, is something that we lost sight of a long time ago. So, it comes as no small surprise when our true King comes calling!

We must understand Jesus' announcement of the Kingdom of God, at least in part, in terms of victory and liberation. Jesus comes as a conquering King, shattering the power of the spiritual forces of evil and liberating men and women from their enslavement to the kingdom of darkness.

The Gospel According To Jesus

Only when we see this aspect of the Kingdom of God do we begin to see the gospel as Jesus proclaimed it. As I said in an earlier chapter, many Christians today see the gospel as forgiveness of their sins so they can live eternally with God. Obviously, forgiveness of sins is important. Jesus didn't die just to show us how much he loved us. He died to pay the consequence of our rebellion, of our high treason against our true King.

But forgiveness is only the starting point. Remember, the Greek word for gospel is *euangelion*; literally, a proclamation of victory over enemies. When Jesus spoke of the good news of the Kingdom, his earliest listeners quite naturally took this as a promise of military victory. That is partially why they wished to crown him as an earthly king (cf. Jn. 6:15), because they expected him to vanquish the Romans and free the nation of Israel from foreign oppression. And Jesus *was* promising a military victory of sorts, but the biblical references to evil spirits and dark kingdoms indicate that he had a very different enemy in view.

The gospel, according to Jesus, was less concerned with the notion of *forgiveness* than it was with the possibility of genuine *freedom*. Again, do not misunderstand me: you cannot enter the Kingdom of God unless you are forgiven of your sins and you cannot be forgiven of your sins apart from placing your faith in the death and resurrection of Christ. But the fact that Christ died for your sins is not the whole story; it is the foyer of the mansion. Even the stupendous fact that he rose from the dead three days later does not completely fill out the whole package.

The gospel according to Jesus, and his earliest followers, was something like this: Good news! By grace, through faith, you can be set free from slavery to the kingdom of darkness and made citizens of the Kingdom of God, and not only citizens, but representatives, royal ambassadors, even, of the King and His Kingdom!

The fact that we are often ignorant of the spiritual reality which under-girds our everyday life does not change the relevance of the gospel today. We are still a people in search of freedom. We are a people who seek freedom with all of our being. We spurn authority; we rebel against rules and restrictions. We claim the freedom to chart our own course and set our own standards. We prize freedom above almost everything else, probably because our rampant individualism forces us to look to liberty as our highest ideal. We are desperate for freedom, but the truth is that we are all too often ignorant of the true source, or nature, of our enslavement. In our ignorance, we often willingly turn from true freedom to a lie.

As a people, and as individuals, we often embrace sin as a defiant claim to autonomy. But what we have achieved is not freedom at all, but a slavery so profound that we can no longer perceive even the machinations of our bondage.

We talk about the "slippery slope" of sin, but I say that sin is not slick. It is sticky. Like Briar Rabbit struggling with the Tar-Baby, our rebellion only mires us deeper and deeper into our slavery. Sin is sticky, but the gospel is slippery. In Christ, we are made slippery with goodness, if you will excuse the odd metaphor. No longer does the dark kingdom have a claim to us and no longer can it hold on to us…every desperate clutch slides harmlessly off, unless we willingly surrender.

The gospel is about freedom: freedom *from* sin and spiritual slavery; freedom *for* a new life as it was meant to be lived in the first place: life as a royal ambassador, a representative of the King and His now-and-coming Kingdom.

Eight

The Now-And-Coming Kingdom

I have, throughout this book, hinted at something which needs now to be addressed explicitly. This issue has caused no small amount of confusion throughout the centuries, for it smacks of the paradoxical. I am referring to the issue of the *timing* of the Kingdom's arrival.

We have already seen that the Kingdom's full arrival does not take place until all things are made new in the new heaven and the new earth. There we will dwell eternally as representatives of our great and glorious King. And yet, as you will have probably noticed already, the Bible does not allow us to think of the Kingdom entirely as a future event. While Scripture is full of references that essentially boil down to the proclamation that the Kingdom is *coming*, it is equally vigorous in its announcement that the Kingdom has already *arrived*.

Jesus himself is probably most responsible for this puzzling state of affairs. On certain occasions, he announced the actual arrival of the Kingdom:

> "But if I cast out demons by the Spirit of God,
> then the kingdom of God *has come* upon you."
> (Matthew 12:28)

> Now having been questioned by the Pharisees as
> to when the kingdom of God was coming, He
> answered them and said, "The kingdom of God
> is not coming with signs to be observed; nor
> will they say, 'Look, here it is!' or, 'There it is!'
> For behold, *the kingdom of God is in your
> midst.*"
>
> (Luke 17:20-21)

The Now-And-Not Yet

It must be noted that such overt statements are somewhat
unusual. However, much of Jesus' Kingdom-talk can only be
heard naturally when we listen to it as descriptions of a *present*
reality:

> "Truly I say to you, among those born of
> women there has not arisen anyone greater than
> John the Baptist! Yet the one who is least in the
> Kingdom of Heaven is greater than he."
>
> (Matthew 11:11)

> But Jesus called for them, saying, "Permit the
> children to come to Me, and do not hinder them,
> for the kingdom of God belongs to such as
> these."
>
> (Luke 18:16)

If the Kingdom were entirely a thing yet to come, we would
expect to find future-tense verbs in such descriptions: "the one
who *will be* least in the Kingdom of Heaven *will be* greater than

he"; "the kingdom of God *will belong* to such as these," etc.[33] And of course we must remember that Jesus had no problem with speaking about the Kingdom as a future reality. It's not as though he made any effort to avoid such references.

Speaking of the Kingdom as a future reality did not at all diminish his proclamation of its present importance. Perhaps this is most clearly illustrated by the parable Jesus told which starts like this:

> While they were listening to these things, Jesus went on to tell a parable, because He was near Jerusalem, and they supposed that the Kingdom of God was going to appear immediately. So He said, "A nobleman went to a distant country to receive a kingdom for himself, and then return."
>
> (Luke 19:11-12)

The clear implication of this parable is that the Kingdom had not yet arrived when Jesus spoke of it. If you are familiar with the rest of the parable - which concerns servants charged with investing the master's money wisely while he was gone –

---

[33] Of course, it is possible that the use of the present tense – or even past tense, as in Mat. 12:28 - is merely a stylistic device; that is, though the Kingdom has not yet actually come, for various rhetorical reasons it was preferable to speak as though it had. I think this unlikely, particularly when we remember that on many occasions, Jesus spoke of the Kingdom specifically as a thing yet to come at some point in the future.

Now, there is, in Greek, a device known as the *proleptic aorist*, in which a verb tense that is generally a reference to past events is used to indicate a future state of affairs that is absolutely, unequivocally, sure to manifest. Whether or not Mat. 12:28 is such a thing or not is a matter of some debate. I am inclined to think that it is not.

then you may already have realized that the parable hints at other things as well. Most Christians understand this parable to be referring to the period between Jesus' Ascension and his Second Coming. If this is the case - and I see no reason to think otherwise - then the parable seems to imply that the Kingdom has still not arrived and will not do so until Jesus himself returns. It is also worth noting that Luke introduced this parable by saying that the disciples "supposed that the Kingdom of God was going to appear immediately." Doesn't this suggest that the disciples thought that the Kingdom had not yet arrived? Of course it does.

So, on the one hand, we have many references to the Kingdom as a future reality. On the other hand, there are good reasons for understanding the Kingdom as a present reality as well. How are we to reconcile these facts?

One option is simply to argue that the Kingdom was present only so long as Jesus was among us. Now that he has gone, the Kingdom has withdrawn as well. This approach might be tempting, but it is difficult to justify in the face of the larger witness of Scripture. First, as we have seen the Kingdom is the sovereign reign of God over and in human affairs and the Church is explicitly identified as the manifestation of this rule during the present age. It will not do to say that the Kingdom has gone simply because Jesus had departed. Second, it is something of an over-simplification to say that Jesus had *departed*. After all, did he not say that the Church is his body, the "fullness of him who fills all in all"? (Eph. 1:23) And does the Spirit not mediate Christ's actual presence to his people? If not, in what sense is Jesus' promise that he would be *"with you always, even to the end of the age"* fulfilled?

To make matters more complicated still, while some references seem to imply that the arrival of the Kingdom was somewhat distant from the perspective of Jesus' earliest followers, other passages virtually require the Kingdom's arrival to have been imminent in the strictest possible sense of the word. Several passages in Scripture describe the Kingdom as *being near, having drawn close,* etc. (cf. Lk. 10:9, 21:31) which all imply the Kingdom's imminent arrival. More to the point, we are forced to contend with enigmatic statements like this one:

> And Jesus was saying to them, "Truly I say to you, there are some of those who are standing here who will not taste death until they see the kingdom of God after it has come with power."
>
> (Mark 9:1)

Our Either/Or vs. God's Both/And

So, where does that leave us? Is the Kingdom a present reality or a future one? Has it come or not?

The answer to all these questions is an emphatic "yes." Is the Kingdom a present reality? Yes. Is the Kingdom a future reality? Yes. Has it come? Yes. Is it still coming? Yes!

Human beings have a predisposition to the either/or. This-not-that depictions of reality fit neatly into our carefully constructed worldviews. We can understand them and apply them. Perhaps more importantly, we can defend them. It's much easier to debate with someone when you can declare his or her view categorically *wrong*. Acknowledge the validity of certain of our opponent's central points, however, and we seem to find ourselves in forensic quicksand, unable to muster a rousing defense. So, whenever possible, we think in terms of the *either/or*.

Unfortunately for our neat packages, God seems to have a predisposition for the *both/and*. There's probably a whole book in the both/ands of God, but for now, we need only acknowledge one of them. As the Bible depicts it, the Kingdom of God is *both* a present *and* a future reality. To put it another way, the Kingdom is now-and-coming.

Now of course, the foundational logical principle of non-contradiction tells us that something cannot be both one thing and the opposite of that thing at the same time and in the same way. For instance, you cannot be both physically alive and physically dead at the same time. It has to be one or the other. This is a basic, apparently unbreakable law of existence[34]. It is as true for God Himself as it is for His creatures. God cannot exist and not exist. God cannot be both good and evil, for evil is the absence of good. Contrary to popular conception, evil is not a thing. It is a "no-thing"; the complete lack of God's character and will.

At first glance, speaking of God's now-and-coming Kingdom seems to be a violation of the law of non-contradiction. However, when we say that God's Kingdom is present, we do not mean that it is here now in precisely the same way that it will be here in the future. This is not a logical absurdity.

Whenever I return from a speaking trip, I am often physically exhausted. The travel, the emotional and spiritual expenditure of energy and the simple fact of being away from my family leaves me worn out and tired. On the other hand, I am often spiritually *refreshed*, having seen God use me in some particularly meaningful way. So, when someone asks me how I am, I frequently respond that I am both weary and refreshed. No one accuses me of being illogical, at least not after I have explained what I mean. Similarly there is no logical problem with saying that a person is both physically dead and yet spiritually alive at the same time.

---

[34] Philosophers sometimes express it this way: A cannot be −A (A cannot be non-A).

So, too, when we describe the Kingdom as now-and-coming, we are not being illogical, for we do not mean that it has *come* and yet is *coming* in precisely the same ways.

The Kingdom has come in several ways that we have already addressed in previous chapters. The Kingdom has come in the sense that God is presently manifesting His reign through the Church. We have, as the book of Hebrews proclaims:

> ...been enlightened and have tasted of the heavenly gift and have been made partakers of the Holy Spirit, and have tasted the good word of God and the powers of the age to come...
>
> (Hebrews 6:4-5)

We have been forgiven, dressed in borrowed robes of righteousness and ushered into the presence of Christ our King.

The Kingdom has come in the sense that believers have been set free from enslavement to the kingdom of darkness and have been restored to their role as representatives of God Almighty. We have been delegated not only the privileges, but also the powers that accompany our office, having authority over evil spirits in the name of Jesus. We no longer answer to the usurper, but to the rightful King.

The Kingdom is here now...but only in *some* ways. In other ways, the Kingdom is yet a future reality.

The Kingdom is now, but the Kingdom is also coming. The Kingdom is coming in the sense that it still awaits at least two important events: the King's return and the people's transformation.

The Kingdom-Now And The Church

Presently, God's rule is being manifest in the Church, but anyone who has ever spent time in a church knows that this rule is not absolute. God's power and presence is, at times, obvious in the Church. Recently, a member of our congregation experienced a traumatic loss of blood following the delivery of her daughter. She went into a coma that lasted for two months. During that time, her family was forced on several occasions to prepare for her death. No one really expected her to recover. If she did somehow regain consciousness, her family was cautioned, it would only be with significant brain damage.

Miraculously (and I do not use the word lightly), she not only regained consciousness but made an almost complete recovery. Unless you knew her well, both before and after the incident, you wouldn't have a clue today what she went through.

God's presence and power during those months were undeniable, in the hospital, in the family and in the life of our church. He manifested Himself in several ways, but one particularly meaningful way was through the Christians who rallied around this woman and her family. So obviously other-worldly was the atmosphere they brought to that hospital that *everyone* noticed.

My wife delivered our second daughter in that same hospital while our friend was still in a coma just a few floors away. As we talked to one of the nurses, this tragedy (which is what it still looked like then) came up. To our surprise and delight, though we hadn't yet told the nurse that we had any connection to this woman, she began telling us that the whole hospital was talking about this woman's incredible church. Of course, not all the Christians who were involved belonged to our congregation, but she didn't know that.

I cannot express the joy we felt in knowing that God's presence was being manifested through His people in such a dramatic way that even non-believers had no choice but to take notice.

The Kingdom-Coming And The Church

That's how it's supposed to be. Unfortunately, it's not always like that. Too often, bitterness, strife, pettiness and selfishness are virtually all that people can see in the Church. For many, the Church is a synonym for corruption and heavy-handed self-righteousness.

In his book, *What's So Amazing About Grace*, Phillip Yancey tells the story of a young woman trapped in a life of sin and despair. When asked why she didn't go to a church for help she choked back her sobs just long enough to spit out, "Why would I go to a church?! I already feel bad enough about myself! They're just going to make me feel even worse." Maybe she was right. Maybe she was wrong. Unfortunately, the fact remains that this is how many people perceive the Church. Why?

The problem is not with the Kingdom itself, of course, but with its citizens. The Kingdom can never operate precisely as it should until its citizens live in a manner worthy of the King whom they represent. Moreover, as we have already seen, it is not always easy to distinguish the true citizens of the Kingdom from the hangers-on; the ones who put up the facades and yet lack the foundations.

In one sense, the Kingdom cannot be said to have fully come until this confusing state of affairs is rectified. Many of Jesus' Kingdom-parables envision precisely this house-cleaning that is still to come:

"Again, the kingdom of heaven is like a dragnet cast into the sea, and gathering fish of every kind; and when it was filled, they drew it up on the beach; and they sat down and gathered the good fish into containers, but the bad they threw away. So it will be at the end of the age; the angels will come forth and take out the wicked from among the righteous, and will throw them into the furnace of fire; in that place there will be weeping and gnashing of teeth."

(Matthew 13:47-50)

"All the nations will be gathered before Him; and He will separate them from one another, as the shepherd separates the sheep from the goats; and He will put the sheep on His right, and the goats on the left. Then the King will say to those on His right, 'Come, you who are blessed of My Father, inherit the kingdom prepared for you from the foundation of the world."

(Matthew 25:32-35)

One of the most intriguing of these parables is the one found in Matthew 13:24-30. There, we are told of a man who planted good seed in his field, but when he looked, found that an enemy had sown weeds among the crop. The man, ostensibly representing God, gave this command to his servants:

"Allow both to grow together until the harvest; and in the time of the harvest I will say to the reapers, 'First gather up the tares and bind them in bundles to burn them up; but gather the wheat into my barn.'"

(Matthew 13:30)

What is intriguing about this parable is the way in which it suggests both the present and the future nature of the Kingdom. When Jesus' disciples later came to him and asked for an explanation of it, he had this to say:

> "The Son of Man will send forth His angels, and they will gather out of His kingdom all stumbling blocks, and those who commit lawlessness, and will throw them into the furnace of fire; in that place there will be weeping and gnashing of teeth."
>
> (Matthew 13:40-42)

Note that this final separation will gather the stumbling blocks and the lawless ones *out of* the Kingdom. This cannot happen, of course, unless the Kingdom is already established in some sense. The Kingdom has to already exist before people can be gathered *out of* it. Indeed, this is precisely what the gospel proclaims: the Kingdom *has come* with power and people may enter into it *now*.

Yet, at the same time, the Kingdom of God, as described consistently in Scripture, is a place/state of perfection, in which the "righteous shine forth as the sun" (Mat. 13:43). In light of this, it doesn't make sense to describe the Kingdom as a mixed-bag of sin and sinless-ness. How can the Kingdom of God contain that which is not of God? It cannot and will not:

> For this you know with certainty, that no immoral or impure person or covetous man, who is an idolater, has an inheritance in the kingdom of Christ and God.
>
> (Ephesians 5:5)

In light of this, we are forced to conclude that the Kingdom has not yet come, or at least is not yet complete. Like a slide being brought into focus, the Kingdom is present, but not yet perfectly clear.

You May Have Won The *War*...

A good friend and trusted mentor of mine once drew a connection between D-Day and the Kingdom's now-and-coming nature. D-Day, of course, June 6, 1944, saw the critically important invasion of Normandy by Allied forces. Most historians are in agreement that this event was the beginning of the end for the Axis powers in Europe at least. From D-Day forward, there was really no question who would win the war. In a very real sense, the war was over...and yet battles remained to be fought. Similarly, with Jesus' incarnation, crucifixion and resurrection, the Kingdom of God has invaded the kingdom of darkness. It is no longer a proxy rule from a distant King, but an imminent reality in the very midst of human existence. In a very real sense, the war is over...but battles remain and a final cleansing still hovers on the horizon of history.

The now-and-coming nature of the Kingdom is mirrored in its King. Jesus has come...yet he is coming again. He has already arrived. He has already shattered the strongholds of darkness, paid the price for sin, and defeated death. In and through the work of the Holy Spirit, he remains with his people. His first coming was not precisely a lightening strike behind enemy lines, followed by a full-scale retreat. He is here and here to stay. Yet, at the same time, he is coming. As the angels told his disciples while they stood watching the sky into which Jesus had bodily ascended: *"he...will come in just the same way as you have watched Him go into heaven."* (Acts 1:11)

We do not await Jesus' *coming*. We are waiting for him to come *back*; to return bodily, with the final, cataclysmic manifestation of the Kingdom of God. He has come and is coming...and so, too, his Kingdom.

The Kingdom of God is like the shock wave of a nuclear bomb. It has detonated and its advance is inexorable; it cannot be stopped, dissuaded, slowed down or escaped. You can run from it, for a while, but it will overtake all things in its time.

NINE

Like A R.O.C.K.
- Living as Representatives Of Christ and his Kingdom -

Not too long ago, I took my daughter, Rochelle, for a walk. She was about three years old at the time. We walked over to a plot of land that my church had purchased for a building project. I was excited about the project. For years, we had met in schools, rented halls and, most recently, in an old office building/strip mall complex. During all that time, the church had grown in spite of our facilities, so it was thrilling to imagine what God would do through us when we had a space that didn't always seem to be working against us.

As we walked over the plot, my daughter asked why we were there. I explained that I just wanted to look at the land because we were going to build a church there. "Really?" she asked. "Here?"

"That's right. Right here."

Rochelle looked around doubtfully. Then she smiled, shrugged and bent down. As I watched, puzzled, she began collecting rocks.

"What are you doing?" I asked.

"Getting rocks," she said patiently, obviously wondering how I could have missed this fact.

"I know. I mean, *why*?"

She looked at me with a bemused expression[35]. "Because you said we were going to build a church," she said.

I stared at her, realization gradually dawning. "Oh," I said. "We are, but I didn't mean right now. I didn't mean you and I were going to build it tonight."

She stared at me. "Why not?" she asked.

"Well, because...um, I guess that..." I trailed off. I suppose I could have explained how complicated a church facility was to build. I could have told her how much time and money it was going to take. I could have tried to enlighten her about site preparation and foundations and civil codes and town approval and all that. But she didn't care. I had said we were going to build a church and she was ready to get started!

If you and I could find even a fraction of that enthusiasm and simplicity of expectation, I could end this book right now. In fact, writing it would probably have been unnecessary.

Like A Child

I believe this sort of thing is largely what Jesus had in mind when he said:

> "Permit the children to come to Me; do not hinder them; for the kingdom of God belongs to such as these. Truly I say to you, whoever does not receive the kingdom of God like a child will not enter it at all."
>
> (Mark 10:14-15)

---

[35] And if you're thinking that a three-year old child cannot adopt a bemused expression, then you obviously have not been around enough three-year olds.

I have heard people say that coming to Jesus like a little child means that we are to lay aside our need to know, to understand, our need to explicate doctrine and split theological hairs. Some of that may be true, I suppose, but anyone who has ever spent any time with children will tell you that their thirst for knowledge is, if anything, less quenchable than ours. They are voracious in their quest to understand and nothing is more frustrating for a child than to be told "You'll understand when you're older." They don't want to understand when they're older. They want to know now.

Nor are children *innocent*, the other popular explanation for Jesus' enigmatic statement. Their schemes may be less complex and narrower in scope, but the endless quest for self-gratification begins very early.

Our first daughter was what they called an "easy" child. From the beginning she seemed to have been a gift from God intended to make people think we were the best parents in the world. She was sociable and amiable. She was flexible. She went on mission trips and slept on hard floors. She never disobeyed[36]. All we had to do was look at her sternly and she burst into tears.

Our second daughter, however, quickly disabused us of any lingering belief that we had somehow spontaneously mastered the art of parenting. With Rochelle, we never even childproofed the house. There was no need. Since Lynae's arrival, however, we have locked down and lifted up and covered over and taken just about every other preventative action you can imagine. And still, it is full-time job just keeping her out of things. Rochelle was destroyed by looks. Lynae thinks stern looks are hilarious. Swat Lynae's hand for repeatedly touching something forbidden and she looks at you with this odd mixture of anger and disbelief as if to say, "You

---

[36] Note the use of the past tense. She didn't stay this way for long!

did *not* just smack my hand!" She didn't learn this from us. She didn't pick it up from her sister. She's simply acting out of a sin nature that she, like all the rest of us, inherited from Adam and Eve. We've all got the same nature…it just comes out in different ways. No one learns how to be sinful, we just learn new and more terrible ways to sin. Anyone who has children can testify to the truth of this long-standing Christian doctrine.

I say that coming to Jesus like a child has little or nothing to do with intellectual quibbling and selflessness and everything to do with enthusiasm. Small children don't do anything half-heartedly. They run, dance, sing and play with abandon. They weep and mourn with a depth that breaks the staunchest of hearts. They know nothing of reserve, of holding back, of biding time. If it's worth doing, it is worth doing *now* and with a vigor that puts the greatest passions of our later years to pitiful shame.

This, I believe, is largely what Jesus had in mind when he spoke those familiar words. Is this not, after all, the kind of behavior that earned from him the greatest praise?

Highest Praise

The Gospel of Matthew tells a story about a woman who could not find relief from her bleeding. Do you remember how she pushed through the crowds, though she knew that her infirmity made her one of the Unclean? If anyone had recognized her and called attention to her presence in the boisterous, bustling, jostling crowd, she would have been stoned to death on the spot. But the hunch that Jesus could help…the hope that he would…in her enthusiasm to reach him, all other considerations were cast aside. And what did he say to her? Simply this:

"Daughter, take courage; your faith has made you well." At once the woman was made well.

(Matthew 9:22)

This is the only time the Gospels ever record Jesus addressing anyone this way. Daughter. A term of intimate familiarity and affection. Why?

And He said to them, "Truly I say to you, there is no one who has left house or wife or brothers or parents or children, for the sake of the kingdom of God, who will not receive many times as much at this time and in the age to come, eternal life."

(Luke 18:29-30)

These are the promises given to those who had pulled their boats up on the shores, dropped their nets, closed down their tax booths and left everything to follow him (Lk. 5:11,27). Similarly, Abraham earned his place in the hall of faith because:

…when he was called, he obeyed by going out to a place which he was to receive for an inheritance; and he went out, not knowing where he was going.

(Hebrews 11:8)

I believe Abraham was not praised for being willing to obey in spite of ignorance, though he was that, but for being willing to obey in spite of all the things of which he was not ignorant; all those things his obedience would cost him. But Abraham did not care. Those things were irrelevant, lost in his enthusiasm to follow the One who called.

I say again that God has always reserved His highest praise, not for faith steeped in *ignorance*, but for faith overflowing with *enthusiasm*. What God desires from us is a trust that knows no reservations and therefore breeds an enthusiasm that knows no boundaries.

Unfortunately, that kind of faith is a flame that is difficult to keep burning. As we age, we grow more cautious, more considered. Over time, our enthusiasm wanes. Our very capacity for it seems to diminish. When was the last time you laughed so hard that you cried? When was the last time you were so excited about something...anything...you couldn't go to sleep or get your work done?

For a while, Rochelle was in such a sweet stage of life. Sometimes I would wake her up in the morning and ask, "How would you like to go on an adventure today?" The answer was always an enthusiastic "yes!" Sometimes she would get so excited she just jumped up and down and squealed. She didn't know what the adventure was yet...and she didn't care. It was an adventure! Daddy said so and that was good enough for her.

We still have adventures, of course, but I can see signs of the enthusiasm slipping away. Now, when I extend the invitation, I am very likely to get contemplation and consideration. "Hmmm," she will often say. "What is it? What are we going to do?"

It's not that she doesn't trust me. She just has her own agenda now. She had things she was planning to do that day and the attraction of her own plans invariably colors the way she sees my invitation.

We're all that way. As we grow older, more "mature," our capacity for wonder and enthusiasm diminishes. It grows brittle with age and we fear to press it too hard.

If we could somehow recapture that childishness, this final chapter would be unnecessary. It wouldn't be needed because, seeing the implications of the now-and-coming Kingdom, we couldn't wait to get to it.

Get to *what*, you ask?

Precisely.

Getting To It

If I give my wife, Coletta, a gift, for instance a necklace, she'll say "I can't wait to wear this!" If I give a necklace to my daughter, Rochelle, she'll ask "When can I where it?" But give a necklace to my youngest daughter, Lynae, and she'll put it on.

If it won't fit over her head, she'll wear it as a headband. If it won't stay there, she'll wrap it around her wrist like a bracelet. She doesn't care about appropriate occasions…she's going to wear it *now*. She doesn't need instructions on its use either. She will accept suggestions, but in the absence of specific ideas, she will find something to do with it.

Most of us aren't like that. New ideas, like gifts, are to be received joyfully and with gratitude to the giver. But more often than not, when the wrapping paper is thrown away and the giver is gone, we stare at the gifts and ask, "What am I going to do with this?"

Francis Schaeffer once wrote a book called *How Should We Then Live?* It is an important question, of course, for to paraphrase Paul, a little knowledge goes a long way towards puffing us up. It will not do to simply discover truth about the Kingdom if we cannot also see how to live differently in light of that knowledge.

So, how should we then live? How should our lives look different for having appropriated theses truths about the Kingdom of God?

Recognizing Our Role As Royal Ambassadors

If you ever have the chance, watch a United Nations formal ceremony. It is fascinating to observe the representatives from various countries as they are announced and enter the room. For the most part, each ambassador receives polite applause..."golf applause," I call it. They enter with calm dignity and take their places quietly.

When the ambassador for the United States is announced, however, the atmosphere changes. People sit up and take notice. The applause is brisker, less lethargic. It goes on for longer. But the most important thing to notice is not the attention the ambassador receives, but the ambassador himself. He enters with his shoulders back and his chin up. He walks with a bounce to his step and an air of authority.

Now, you may attribute this to arrogance. You might even be right to some extent, but it matters little. What matters is that our ambassadors carry themselves differently not because of who they are, but because of whom they *represent*: the United States of America; the most powerful and prosperous nation on the face of the earth.

And yet, these men and women have nothing on us. We have been made in the very Image of God, fashioned to represent the Almighty. We have been delegated power and authority such that our lives are imbued with a purpose that is almost terrifying to consider. None of us are peasants. From the most sanctified saint to the most pitiful sinner, we are all royal ambassadors...made to represent God not as inanimate sculptures, but as beings who are genuinely like Him in real and tangible ways; or at least, as beings who have that *potential*. We all have royal blood, but this is no guarantee of regality.

C.S. Lewis seems to have had something of this fact in mind when, in The Weight of Glory, he stated:

> It is a serious thing to live in a society of
> possible gods and goddesses, to remember that
> the dullest and most uninteresting person you
> may talk to may one day be a creature which, if
> you saw it now, you would be strongly tempted
> to worship, or else a horror and corruption such
> as you now meet if at all only in a nightmare.

If this fact does not change the way we see ourselves...and
the way we see everyone around us, then we are beyond the
pale of hope.

God's plan for us is awesome. There is no other word for it.
He has made us for a purpose that confounds comprehension.
For, while it is true that He has made us like Him in some
respects, to call us gods and goddesses, as Lewis does, is to
latch onto those words only in their thinnest possible sense.
We are like Him, but He is not very much like us. That we
should be entrusted with the sacred task of representing such as
He...surely we cannot think on this without seizing the
psalmist's words for our own:

> What is man that You take thought of him,
> And the son of man that You care for him?
> Yet You have made him a little lower than God,
> And You crown him with glory and majesty!
> You make him to rule over
> the works of Your hands;
> You have put all things under his feet,
> All sheep and oxen,
> And also the beasts of the field,
> The birds of the heavens and the fish of the sea,
> Whatever passes through the paths of the seas.

O LORD, our Lord,
How majestic is Your name in all the earth!
(Psalm 8:4-9)

Before anyone objects that I have suggested here a too-lofty view of humanity, let me point out two things. First, I think that I am not saying anything more boldly than the Scripture itself declares. Second, there is no glory inherent to us. What glory may accrue to us is not radiated, but *reflected*, as the moon blazes in the night sky not because of its own light but because of the sun's. We are not glorious, but God is, and we were made to reflect His glory brilliantly.

Ironically, is our staggering potential that makes us so often despicable. We revel in our rebellion, renegade ambassadors who have sold the privileges of our position for cheap thrills, like royals who have gone a-whoring. We not only choose sin, we declare it our *right*...and righteous. Daily, concerning our imagined sovereignty over our own lives, we all declare with Nebuchadnezzer:

> "Is this not Babylon the great, which I myself
> have built as a royal residence by the might of
> my power and for the glory of my majesty?"
> (Daniel 4:30)

The Church, too, forgets itself. We so often fail to live in the knowledge that we have been given the inconceivable privilege of living every moment of every day as representatives, royal ambassadors, of the King and His Kingdom. At present, the Church is the manifestation of the Kingdom of God. We are supposed to be the living, breathing, in-their-faces reminder that there is a King and He is coming.

The Church is supposed to be about the business of being filled and spilled...about being so filled with the presence, love, knowledge and *enthusiasm* that comes from knowing God and His Word, that it has to spill out of us onto the culture around us. The world should not be able to look at the Church without hearing the sound of trumpets and knowing that the King is coming…that He's already here in the lives of His people…in the Church.

Conclusion

How do we do that? How can you, personally, put that into practice?

There is no single answer to such a question. How we do it as a Church and as individuals must inevitably flow out of our realization of who God is and who we are made and called to be in relation to Him. We could say things like "sin less" or "cherish your neighbor more" and so on, but we've already been told such things countless times. The issue isn't so much *what* we are supposed to do but *why* we are supposed to do it.

If you desire to live radically, love deeply and serve sacrificially, if you want to be everything that you were made to be and everything that God desires to transform you into, then there is only one option. You must let the Kingdom invade your life as it has invaded human history. You must abdicate the throne of your life and install there the rightful King. You must begin to look at everything through a new lens; that of the realization that in Christ you have been adopted into the King's family *and* sent out to represent Him to a desperate and watching world. We have been filled so that we can be spilled.

Only when we begin to live every moment of every day in light of these facts can we ever expect our lives to become a living proclamation of the now-and-coming Kingdom and its now-and-coming King.

Amen.

INDEX OF SUBJECTS

INDEX OF SCRIPTURE AND ANCIENT SOURCES

Craig is a popular retreat and conference speaker. If you are interested in booking him for a speaking engagement, contact:

Shepherd Project Ministries
720.231.7579
www.shepherdproject.com